S0-CFD-348

the easy and healthy slow cooker cookbook

Incredibly Simple
Prep-and-Go
Whole Food Meals

THE
easy & healthy
SLOW COOKER
COOKBOOK

SHANNON
EPSTEIN

ROCKRIDGE
PRESS

Copyright © 2017 by Shannon Epstein

No part of this publication may be reproduced, stored in a retrieval system or transmitted in any form or by any means, electronic, mechanical, photocopying, recording, scanning or otherwise, except as permitted under Sections 107 or 108 of the 1976 United States Copyright Act, without the prior written permission of the Publisher. Requests to the Publisher for permission should be addressed to the Permissions Department, Rockridge Press, 918 Parker St, Suite A-12, Berkeley, CA 94710.

Limit of Liability/Disclaimer of Warranty: The Publisher and the author make no representations or warranties with respect to the accuracy or completeness of the contents of this work and specifically disclaim all warranties, including without limitation warranties of fitness for a particular purpose. No warranty may be created or extended by sales or promotional materials. The advice and strategies contained herein may not be suitable for every situation. This work is sold with the understanding that the publisher is not engaged in rendering medical, legal or other professional advice or services. If professional assistance is required, the services of a competent professional person should be sought. Neither the Publisher nor the author shall be liable for damages arising herefrom. The fact that an individual, organization or website is referred to in this work as a citation and/or potential source of further information does not mean that the author or the Publisher endorses the information the individual, organization or website may provide or recommendations they/it may make. Further, readers should be aware that Internet websites listed in this work may have changed or disappeared between when this work was written and when it is read.

For general information on our other products and services or to obtain technical support, please contact our Customer Care Department within the U.S. at (866) 744-2665, or outside the U.S. at (510) 253-0500.

Rockridge Press publishes its books in a variety of electronic and print formats. Some content that appears in print may not be available in electronic books, and vice versa.

TRADEMARKS: Rockridge Press and the Rockridge Press logo are trademarks or registered trademarks of Callisto Media Inc. and/or its affiliates, in the United States and other countries, and may not be used without written permission. All other trademarks are the property of their respective owners. Rockridge Press is not associated with any product or vendor mentioned in this book.

Photograph of the author © Joshua Monesson, Monesson Photography

Photography © Jennifer Davick, cover & pp. ii & v; Ruth Küng/Stockfood, p. vi; Pixel Stories/Stocksy, p. xii; The Picture Pantry/Stockfood, p. xiv; Natasa Mandic/Stocksy, pp. 14, 158 & back cover; Jana Liebenstein/Gräfe & Unzer Verlag/Stockfood, p. 30; Julia Hoersch/Jalag/Stockfood, p. 52 & back cover; Gareth Morgans/Stockfood, p. 74; Tanya Zouev/Stockfood, pp. 92 & 140; Great Stock!/Stockfood, p. 114.

Title spread photograph: Tex-Mex Chicken Soup *page 35*

ISBN: Print 978-1-62315-967-2
eBook 978-1-62315-968-9

For Zulu
(200?–2016)

contents

4 pasta, rice, and other grains   53

5 beans, lentils, and vegetables   75

introduction

When most people think about slow cooker recipes, *healthy* isn't the first thing that comes to mind. I understand that perception, but I'm out to change it.

I received my first slow cooker in late 2011 as a wedding present. At that time I had also just started a new job, which required long hours in the office or out on the road. While I managed to keep physically active, my diet took a beating. I ate out more than ever, and within six months I found myself at my all-time highest weight—I called it my *wedding weight*. I knew that 50 percent of losing weight and staying fit and healthy day to day comes down to diet, so I broke out my slow cooker and turned to the Internet for inspiration. To say I was disappointed was an understatement. While I found tons of slow cooker recipes, I was shocked at how obviously unhealthy most of them were. I was expecting to see recipes made from fresh, natural ingredients, but most were high in fat and sodium, loaded with butter, flavored with premade seasoning packets, or full of processed foods like those canned "cream of" soups.

I decided to ditch other people's recipes and concentrate on making my own from scratch, using natural ingredients. I soon realized that healthy cooking can taste fantastic! Within eight weeks I had lost that wedding weight and more, and I haven't looked back since. These days I use my slow cooker on average five times a week. Most days I just throw in a protein, a starch, some vegetables, and a homemade sauce. The combinations are endless—as long as you start with fresh, natural foods.

Slow cookers allow even the busiest of people to produce delicious, hands-off meals—but to make them healthy, you need to put in a little extra effort. I understand that in a way, this seems like a contradiction. After all, we associate slow cookers with recipes that are "dump and go"—you know, ingredients you can throw into the pot with no other preparation required, and simply come home to a finished meal. You might think that taking the time to create your own healthy seasoning blends or sauces defeats the convenience of slow cooking. However, with a bit of time management, I think you'll find that the prep needed is still very minimal compared to other cooking methods.

To me, the key to healthy slow cooker meals lies in making your own sauces, seasonings, and spice blends. Homemade seasonings and spice blends are great for maximizing flavor without adding calories, because most spices contain little to no calories. And you probably have all the spices you need in your pantry already. I like to store big batches of my favorite go-to blends like Taco Seasoning (page 51) and Italian Seasoning (page 100) so they're ready when I need them. When it comes to homemade sauces, water or vinegar provide great, healthy bases. Just a little water, vinegar, a healthy oil like extra-virgin olive oil, and spices can produce a winning sauce. I'll explain exactly how I do it and provide recipes for popular sauces like Barbecue Sauce (page 124), Salsa Verde (page 116), and Enchilada Sauce (page 62).

Let's keep it real. Cooking every single meal, every single day can be hard for most people. Most likely, they don't have the time, don't know how to cook, or both. But with healthy ingredients and a slow cooker, you can solve both problems! And simple substitutions can easily turn a heavy slow cooker recipe into a light and healthy version. For example, rather than using canned beans, buy dried beans. Not only do they cost less, but they contain a third of the sodium content. You can even use your slow cooker to soak the beans overnight.

Throughout this book, I'll explain which food combinations are best suited for slow cooking. I'll also give you basic formulas to use so you can whip up super-quick healthy recipes that don't compromise on flavor. At the same time, I've made sure that all the recipes are low in calories yet hearty enough to provide a full meal on their own (many include a protein, vegetables, and starch all in a single recipe) or when paired with a side salad. Best of all, unlike many slow cooker recipes calling for extensive prep, most of these recipes require less than 15 minutes to prepare the ingredients, with little to no precooking requirements, and then cook low and slow all day. When you arrive home in the evening, your one-pot meal will be ready to enjoy.

CHAPTER 1

healthy at its *easiest*

While there's really no excuse for unhealthy eating, making sure to eat consistently nutritious meals can certainly present some challenges. It's important both to understand which foods you should be eating and then to take the time to prepare them in a healthy manner. The problem is that cooking wholesome, nonprocessed food for yourself (and others) every day can be both time-consuming and tiring. And we're all busy. No one wants to spend a lot time in the kitchen after working all day. Even those who have mastered meal prep can spend hours in the kitchen between chopping and other tasks to prep and cook various foods. Furthermore, food is not necessarily cheap—at least not the nutritious foods we should be eating. The cost of fresh, natural ingredients for recipes can add up, specifically when they're specialty items you'll use only occasionally. Here too, slow cookers can help, using less expensive ingredients. Most people don't realize how great slow cookers are for producing cost-effective, healthy meals with a minimal amount of work. In short, the slow cooker can play a key role in helping you lead a healthy lifestyle.

the perfect pair

The slow cooker equals healthy eating made easy. This amazing appliance provides the solution to many issues of both nutrition and convenience. First off, slow cooking as a technique is incredibly easy. Though not necessarily the case for all slow cooker recipes, those in this book let you throw all the ingredients into the pot at the beginning of the day and walk away. That's it: Then you simply come home to a delicious meal. And whole, uncut foods and meats are perfect for the slow cooker. And did I mention that your kitchen, if not your entire house, will smell amazing?

Cooks While You're Away

Set it and forget it—that's pretty much the slow cooker motto. I believe that if you know you're going to come home to an appetizing home-cooked meal, you're less likely to opt for takeout or find yourself eating unhealthy, processed foods. The concept of leaving your food to cook and walking away is undeniably convenient.

You Control the Ingredients

Slow cookers give you more control over what you're eating, resulting in both healthier and cheaper meals. Fresh ingredients work exceptionally well in the slow cooker. Use fresh vegetables, fresh starches like sweet potatoes, and pretty much any cut of meat—the tougher, the better. Slow cookers also encourage you to use less expensive ingredients. For example, using dried beans you've soaked overnight rather than higher-sodium canned beans is not only better for you but cheaper, too.

Low and Slow

Set to the right temperature, slow cooking will cook vegetables to perfection, and starches as well—potatoes cooked just right, that a fork pierces easily. Ever had meat so tender it literally melts in your mouth? If not, you haven't tried

SLOW COOKER OR CROCK-POT?

Slow cooker is the generic name for an appliance that has heating elements in a metal housing around an insert and can be safely left unattended on your countertop as it slowly cooks a meal. *Crock-Pot* is the Rival Company's registered trademark for its slow cookers. The terms "slow cooker" and "Crock-Pot" are often used interchangeably, much like "tissue" and "Kleenex." While all Crock-Pots are slow cookers, not all slow cookers are Crock-Pots. Other popular slow cooker brands include All-Clad, Cuisinart, and Hamilton Beach. Even the popular Instant Pot pressure cooker has a slow cooker function.

slow-cooked meat. Even the toughest meats will become tender during the low-and-slow cooking process to the point that they shred with a fork. Using tough cuts has health benefits, too: They are generally lower in fat, decreasing the overall fat and calorie content of slow cooker meals.

Healthier and Safer Cooking Method

Some people worry about slow cookers stripping the nutrients out of food. But this couldn't be further from the truth. Cooking food at low temperatures for a long period of time preserves nutrients normally lost at high temperatures. Slow cooking also eliminates the risk of AGEs (advanced glycation end products) occurring when foods are cooked at high heat.

Year-Round Cooking

Can't stand a hot kitchen in the middle of the summer? Prefer not to grill in the winter? The slow cooker solves both these problems. You can cook the same wholesome meals without changing your cooking methods or ingredients. And in general, slow cookers use substantially less energy than a conventional electric oven.

healthy eating guidelines

Healthy eating means different things to different people. Your concept of healthy may have little in common with the next person's, depending on a variety of possible issues such as food allergies, a medical condition, or even your living environment. While there's no wrong answer, this cookbook focuses on providing basic recipes that use nutrient-rich, whole food ingredients and avoid processed foods, refined sugars, and artificial additives. I understand that people's needs can be widely different, so I tried to cater to as many different dietary requirements as possible in these recipes, whether they be for foods that are gluten-free, vegan/vegetarian, Paleo, dairy-free—you get my drift.

Choose High-Fiber Carbohydrates

Carbs are okay! I'm talking about good carbs, or non-refined carbs, which have tons of nutritional benefits. They assist with brain function, help speed up metabolism, provide energy, and aid with sleep, digestion, and more. You're probably more familiar with non-refined carbs than you realize. They include foods such as lentils, black beans, quinoa, split peas, whole-wheat pasta, barley, oatmeal, chickpeas, and chia seeds (also a superfood). These are also great sources of fiber, another essential component of our diets. A high-fiber diet helps protect against numerous medical conditions, such as cancer, diabetes, and heart disease.

Avoid Sugar

Sugar, on the other hand, is one of the "bad carbs," or a refined carbohydrate. Refined sugar has no nutritional value in itself, yet it's found in almost all processed foods, usually hidden so you don't know how much you are consuming. So rather than buying a bottle of salad dressing or a jar of salsa verde, make your own. All the sauces in this cookbook are homemade. They include nothing processed and absolutely no added sugar—you will not see the word *sugar* listed on a single ingredient list here. I don't even use sugar in my dessert recipes. Even natural sweeteners like honey I use sparingly; however, unlike refined sugar, honey has nutritional value and benefits to your health.

Limit Sodium

As with sugar, I don't believe in adding lots of sodium to meals. Don't get me wrong, a little salt in moderation is okay, and it certainly adds flavor to a dish. However, sodium chloride (salt) has long been linked to high blood pressure, or hypertension. It affects nearly one in three Americans and is a leading cause of heart disease. I have a family history of heart disease, so I've seen how a low-sodium lifestyle can literally change lives. An effective way to immediately lower your sodium intake (as with sugar) is to eliminate processed foods and start reading labels. Avoiding sodium completely can sometimes be impossible; however, you can make small changes. For example, use low-sodium broth when making soups or stews—you can cut as much as 500 to 900 milligrams of sodium per serving. And use dried beans rather than canned. Canned beans usually contain added salt and therefore hundreds of milligrams of sodium.

the right slow cooker

As you can imagine, I have a lot of slow cookers. I currently have six (all different brands) in my home! I have pretty much every size—some programmable, some manual. And yes, I use them all! These different sizes and brands serve different functions. Having said that, I understand that most people will not need this many—six is a lot. If you do a lot of slow cooking I recommend two, but even one is enough. I tend to use a programmable 6-quart slow cooker the most. I cook for four most nights, so I need the 6-quart size, and I'm usually not home when the food finishes cooking, so I need the programmable function that will switch to warm, so the food doesn't overcook. In the following sections I explain what you should look for when choosing a slow cooker, whether for your own home or as a gift for someone else.

Size

The most important factor in choosing a slow cooker is size. In general, slow cookers come in the following sizes: less than 2 quarts; 3½ quarts; 4, 5, or 6 quarts; and 7 quarts or larger. If you're feeding just one or two people, you'll never need more than a 3½-quart model. To feed three to five people, you'll need a 4- to 6-quart cooker. If you plan to cook for any more people than this, you'll need a 7-quart cooker or larger, or look into purchasing two. To test the recipes for this book, I used a 6-quart cooker. The one thing you want to avoid is a slow cooker that's too big for the amount of food you're cooking. If you don't fill the cooker to at least 75 percent of its capacity, you risk burning the food.

Shape

The basic slow cooker shapes are oval and round, and now there are even some oblong or square casserole-shaped models. I cook a lot of simple one-pot meals, so to me the shape doesn't really matter as long as the size is right. However, the

NO PROGRAMMABLE SLOW COOKER?

If you already own a manual slow cooker and you don't feel you are ready to upgrade to a programmable one quite yet, another alternative is to invest in a digital electric socket timer. This way your slow cooker will shut off automatically after it has completed cooking, rather than continuing to cook your food all day. You can pick up a socket timer at your hardware store for less than $10. It's simple to use: Just plug the timer into the outlet, plug your slow cooker into the timer, and then set the timer to cook for the appropriate time. To avoid any chance of harmful bacteria growing on room-temperature food, don't set the timer to begin any later than two hours after putting the food in the slow cooker, and don't let the completed dish stand in the slow cooker for any longer than two hours (and no longer than one hour at a room temperature over 90°F).

different shapes can come in handy depending on your needs. What will you be cooking? Breads and cakes cook better in oval-shaped cookers, but round cookers are usually less expensive. Round cookers tend to cook a bit more unevenly, but for one-pot meals they're fine. Do you cook mainly casseroles or whole cuts of meat? If you will need to fit large cuts of meat (think: whole chicken), an oval is probably more practical. Also consider storage: Will your slow cooker be stored on the countertop or in the pantry? Will it fit there if it's round? Choose the slow cooker that works best for your purposes and your space.

Features

Programmable or manual? As I said, I have both. Programmable cookers are a little more expensive, but for me, it's worth the investment. In addition to the usual high, low, and warm settings, a programmable slow cooker has a timer that allows you to set the actual cook time. Once the cook time has completed, the slow cooker automatically turns to warm until you turn it off. That way, the food will remain heated without overcooking. A new feature offered by some slow cooker brands is a sear option, so you can sear the meat directly in its base rather than on the stove.

easy, essential prep

Slow cooker prep falls into two categories: essential and optional. Essential prep refers to techniques like chopping vegetables or cutting up the meat before you add it to the slow cooker. Optional steps are methods like sautéing vegetables or browning meat before adding them to the slow cooker. I try to keep my recipes as easy as possible, so most of the recipes you find here do not require any optional steps. However, if you have the time for this pre-step, I recommend you do so. Browning ground meat or sautéing vegetables such as onions, garlic, and mushrooms on the stove top not only adds flavor, but it also allows you to discard all the grease before you add the food to the slow cooker.

healthy favorites–and what to forget

Some foods are great for the low-and-slow method, while others are admittedly a flat-out disaster. For example, brisket is one of the toughest cuts of beef you can buy, but cooked in the slow cooker, it can become one of the most succulent. The flip side is that filet mignon, arguably one of the choicest meats, is totally wasted in the slow cooker. It cooks too fast and quickly becomes overcooked. Similarly, root vegetables work great, but leafy vegetables not so much! Below are some ingredients that are perfect for slow cooking and others that are best to avoid.

Favorites

Cheap Cuts of Meat The low-and-slow method of cooking meat makes even the toughest cut melt-in-your-mouth tender. Some cheap cuts of meat that work particularly well are beef brisket, corned beef, skirt steak, pork cheek, and chicken thighs.

Large Cuts of Meat As long as it fits in the slow cooker and you have the time, the meat will cook perfectly—all you need is patience. Cooked long enough, even the largest cut of pork or beef will cook to the point of being so tender it will shred with a fork. Examples of such large cuts include beef top, bottom or round, pork shoulder, and lamb shoulder.

Potatoes Never worry about over- or undercooking your potatoes again. Whether you're wrapping them in foil for a basic baked potato/sweet potato or peeling them for some mashed, your slow cooker provides a foolproof method to cook them to perfection.

Root Vegetables Root vegetables such as carrots and parsnips are ideal for the slow cooker because they require a longer cooking method to reach doneness and won't turn to mush like more tender vegetables.

Dried Beans Using dried beans in your slow cooker meals provides many benefits. First off, they're healthier than canned beans. They also hold their form better and are less likely to turn to mush if slightly overcooked. They're cheaper, too, and you can even soak them in the slow cooker overnight first.

Fresh Herbs Herbs can add tons of flavor to slow cooker meals. Whenever possible, use fresh herbs—not only is the aroma stronger, but they also add a creative finishing touch. Whenever a recipe calls for fresh herbs, I make sure to reserve some for the garnish.

Grains Traditionally long-cooking grains such as barley, steel-cut oatmeal, and wild rice cook perfectly in the slow cooker. These ingredients are ideal for overnight slow cooker recipes.

Canned Tomato Products From diced tomatoes to stewed tomatoes, embrace the cans. Canned tomatoes make a great staple ingredient for slow cooker casseroles, stews, and roasts.

Low-Sodium Broth Let's face it, you can't have a soup or stew without broth. Ideally, we'd all make our own broths all the time, but that's not realistic. Good-quality low-sodium broth is readily available at supermarkets nationwide. (For information on purchasing, or making, gluten-free broth, see A Word on Store-Bought Broth on page 13.)

Forget It

Seafood Seafood cooks very quickly—I'm talking 15 to 30 minutes—in the slow cooker, so in most cases, seafood should be added at the end of the cook time. Since this pretty much violates the whole slow-cooking concept of "set it and forget it," there are no seafood recipes in this book.

Filet Mignon or Other Lean Cuts Lean meats like sirloin steak and chicken breast are simply not meant for the slow cooker. Save those expensive cuts for another method. They just cook too quickly and thus are especially difficult to use when cooking other foods along with them.

Delicate Vegetables Delicate vegetables make poor slow cooker ingredients because they're just that: too delicate. Save them for your side salad instead!

Alcohol Alcohol needs to evaporate when you cook with it. If you add alcohol to the slow cooker and then put on the lid, it becomes trapped, with no way to evaporate. The result is an unpleasant flavor, so it's best to avoid adding booze.

healthy slow cooker tips

If you follow these basic slow cooker tips, you're almost guaranteed to create a delicious and healthy slow cooker meal:

1. **Select the right size slow cooker.** Using a too large or too small slow cooker is a surefire way to under- or overcook your food.

2. **Cut food uniformly.** Equal-size pieces ensure evenly cooked food. This is particularly important when cutting potatoes and other vegetables.

3. **Trim the fat.** Because meat will be falling-off-the-bone tender once it's cooked, the fat will be almost impossible to remove at that point. Save yourself the trouble and trim the fat before adding the meat to the slow cooker.

4. **Don't overcrowd the slow cooker.** Another surefire way to improperly cook your food is to overstuff the slow cooker. If you're making chili for six, don't use a slow cooker for two.

5. **Add citrus for color and flavor.** Citrus juice and zest contribute not only a dash of color but also refreshing taste to most slow cooker recipes.

6. **Set the timer or plan accordingly.** No one likes overcooked meat! If you don't have a programmable slow cooker, invest in an electric timer so the slow cooker will shut off, or manually turn the cooker to warm after the allocated cook time.

7. **Don't remove the lid.** Slow cookers truly do work best when you leave them be, so just "set and forget." Lifting the lid, even just briefly, can release so much heat that you may need to add an additional 30 minutes of cook time.

SLOW COOKER TEMPERATURES

Ever wonder why slow cooker recipes usually give a range for the cooking time? That's because every slow cooker brand and size cooks differently. It's just the way it is; there's no way around it. I have one slow cooker that will cook food fully in six hours, while another of the same size takes nine. Get to know your slow cooker. The more you use it, the better you'll get to know its heating mechanism. For most of the recipes in this book, I used my 6-quart Hamilton Beach Set & Forget Programmable Slow Cooker with Temperature Probe. It's my go-to slow cooker when I need a 6-quart. When cooking smaller size portions, I used my 3½-quart Cuisinart PSC-350 Programmable Slow Cooker.

about the recipes

The overall theme of this cookbook is to be "comfortably healthy" while offering a healthy take on slow cooking. I'm not trying to take anyone out of their comfort zone. Having said that, I hope to broaden your horizons just a little bit.

In this cookbook, you'll find a wide portfolio of flavors and cuisines, from traditional Indian dishes made healthy, like Paleo Butter Chicken (page 108), to Mexican favorites like Carne Asada (page 132). Some recipes are classics that I've refashioned to be as nutritious as possible without losing their core flavor, such as Lamb Shepherd's Pie (page 138), Old-School Chicken Noodle Soup (page 57), and Low-Carb Paleo Cabbage Rolls (page 129). There's also a chapter on rice, pasta, and grains, so yes, I include carbohydrates—high-fiber carbs. You'll find lots of nutritious soups and stews, along with appetizing meat, poultry, and vegetables dishes, and even tempting sweets. There's everything here from breakfasts using superfoods like sweet potatoes and chia seeds, to flavorful chilies, curries, and casseroles, to hearty vegetarian meals featuring protein-packed lentils, quinoa, and beans, and even sugar-free jams. And yes, all of these can be made in a slow cooker!

Most recipes you find here are meant to be served as complete meals in themselves, though you might want to pair some of them with a salad or vegetable side. It was also important to me to keep prep to a minimum, so you won't find a recipe with a prep time over 15 minutes—and even that's stretching it. Only a handful of recipes require pre-browning or pan-searing (although you're welcome to add these steps to other recipes whenever you have the time and inclination). These are seriously quick and easy recipes: Simply add ingredients to the pot and set to cook—then come home to a delectable dinner eight hours later. That is, except for the breakfast and dessert recipes. I've also suggested a 5 to 7 hour cook time for most chicken recipes, as chicken tends to get a bit rubbery when cooked in the slow cooker for over 8 hours.

While keeping flavor a priority, all recipes here are 600 calories or less, with lots of options in the 200- to 300-calorie range. (Remember we're talking complete meals here!) In addition, all recipes include labels that indicate which dishes are Gluten-Free, Vegan or Vegetarian, Paleo, and Dairy-Free.

A WORD ON STORE-BOUGHT BROTH

Many of the recipes in this book include low-sodium broth as an ingredient. If you follow a gluten-free diet, it's essential that you use gluten-free broth. Some store-bought broths are gluten-free, but not all, so be sure you check the label before using. Hidden gluten, usually in the form of wheat, will appear on the ingredients list. Your safest bet, however, is to make your own. Use this simple recipe for homemade slow cooker broth.

beef or chicken bone broth

SERVES 6 TO 8 / COOK TIME: 8 TO 10 HOURS ON LOW

GLUTEN-FREE • PALEO • DAIRY-FREE

2 pounds beef or chicken bones

2 or 3 celery stalks, chopped

2 or 3 carrots, chopped

1 onion, chopped

5 garlic cloves, minced

2 tablespoons distilled white vinegar

1 teaspoon salt

1 teaspoon freshly ground
   black pepper

1 bay leaf

1. Combine all the ingredients in the slow cooker.
2. Add enough water to cover all the ingredients.
3. Cover and cook on low for 8 to 10 hours.
4. Strain the broth into a container, let cool, cover, and refrigerate.
5. If there's a layer of fat on top of the broth the next morning, remove as much of it as possible and discard. Store the broth in the refrigerator for up to 2 weeks or in the freezer for up to 2 months.

PER SERVING Calories: 82; Total Fat: 3g; Saturated Fat: 1g; Protein: 4g; Carbohydrates: 0g; Cholesterol: 0mg; Sodium: 388mg; Fiber: 0g; Sugar: 0g

Tip: Don't throw bones away! Left-over bones (such as a whole chicken carcass) are great to use in slow cooker broth. You can reuse the bones for at least two batches of broth.

5-Ingredient Strawberry-Basil Chia Seed Jam *page 16*

breakfast
and brunch

....

5-ingredient strawberry-basil chia seed jam

SERVES 6 / COOK TIME: 2 TO 4 HOURS ON LOW

GLUTEN-FREE • VEGETARIAN • PALEO • DAIRY-FREE

When I first started slow cooking, creating a healthy jam with no added sugar was at the top of my list. I soon discovered that not only is this possible, but all you need are a few simple ingredients—five, to be exact. Chia seeds are both a nutritious superfood and a great thickening agent. The recipe calls for 1 tablespoon of chia seeds; you can lower that to 2 teaspoons if you prefer your jam slightly less thick. You can also control the texture: either keep chunks of fruit, or blend until smooth. Honey in place of sugar provides the perfect sweetener.

1 pound fresh strawberries, hulled and sliced

1 tablespoon chia seeds

1 tablespoon honey

1 teaspoon freshly squeezed lemon juice

Handful fresh basil, chopped

....

PER SERVING Calories: 42; Total Fat: 1g; Saturated Fat: 0g; Protein: 1g; Carbohydrates: 10g; Cholesterol: 0mg; Sodium: 1mg; Fiber: 2g; Sugar: 7g

1. Combine all the ingredients in the slow cooker and mix well.

2. Cover and cook on low for 2 to 4 hours. It's done when the strawberries are soft.

3. Using an immersion blender, potato masher, or a spoon, mash the jam until it reaches your desired consistency.

4. Transfer the jam to a Mason jar or other container. Cool, cover, and store in the refrigerator for up to 2 weeks.

Tip: If you prefer not to use any added sweetener—not even honey—add 3 or 4 small pitted dates. You can also swap out the strawberries for another berry of your choice. I encourage you to get creative and start combining fruits—strawberry-blueberry, for example, makes a great jam.

5-ingredient apple butter

SERVES 6 / COOK TIME: 4 TO 6 HOURS ON LOW

GLUTEN-FREE • VEGAN • PALEO

The warm aroma of apples and cinnamon, or "the smell of autumn" as I like to call it, will fill your house when you make this recipe. There are tons of apple butter recipes out there, but most of them use sugar, while this version is sugar-free. An optional but suggested ingredient is ghee, a lactose-free, clarified form of butter that adds creaminess to the recipe. Of course, ghee is not for everyone (such as vegans). Though considered a "good fat," ghee is high in saturated fat, so if you have high cholesterol, you might want to steer clear. However, do not substitute regular butter, or your apple butter will no longer have the same healthy properties.

3 pounds apples, cored

2 teaspoons ground cinnamon

1 tablespoon apple cider vinegar

¼ teaspoon ground nutmeg

1 teaspoon ghee (optional)

. . . .

PER SERVING Calories: 61; Total Fat: 0g; Saturated Fat: 0g; Protein: 0g; Carbohydrates: 16g; Cholesterol: 0mg; Sodium: 1mg; Fiber: 3g; Sugar: 12g

1. Combine all the ingredients in the slow cooker and mix well.

2. Cover and cook on low for 4 to 6 hours, or until the apples are soft.

3. Use an immersion blender or food processor to blend until it reaches your desired consistency.

4. Transfer the apple butter to a Mason jar or other container. Cool, cover, and store in the refrigerator for up to 2 weeks.

Tip: Any type of apple will do. I prefer sweeter apples like Gala or Red Delicious. You don't even need to peel the apples! The skin will become extremely soft once it's cooked—you won't even realize it's there.

dried fruit and nut granola

SERVES 6 / COOK TIME: 6 HOURS ON LOW

GLUTEN-FREE • VEGETARIAN • DAIRY-FREE

When most people think of granola, they think healthy. Unfortunately, when it comes to the store-bought kind, that's not necessarily the case. A lot of store-bought granola is covered in sugar—not to mention a bunch of unnatural stuff I can't even pronounce. Making your own granola not only lets you control the quality of the ingredients, it's also a lot cheaper and is super-easy to prepare in the slow cooker.

Cooking spray

3 cups old-fashioned rolled oats

2 cups almonds, pecans, or walnuts

¼ cup unsweetened coconut flakes

½ cup dried cranberries, berries, or cherries

¼ cup chia seeds

1 teaspoon ground cinnamon

½ teaspoon salt

¼ teaspoon ground nutmeg

¼ cup coconut oil

½ cup honey or maple syrup

1 teaspoon vanilla extract

. . . .

PER SERVING Calories: 539; Total Fat: 34g; Saturated Fat: 16g; Protein: 10g; Carbohydrates: 55g; Cholesterol: 0mg; Sodium: 200mg; Fiber: 8g; Sugar: 31g

Tip: This recipe has infinite variations— use any of your preferred nuts and seeds or dried fruits. If you don't want to use honey or maple syrup, chopped pitted dates provide a great natural sweetener.

1. Coat the inside of the slow cooker generously with cooking spray.

2. Combine the oats, nuts, coconut flakes, dried fruit, chia seeds, cinnamon, salt, and nutmeg in the slow cooker.

3. In a medium bowl, melt the coconut oil in the microwave. Whisk in the honey and vanilla.

4. Pour the mixture into the slow cooker, stirring to make sure all the ingredients are coated.

5. Lay a dish towel or one to two paper towels between the slow cooker and the lid. This will absorb all the condensation so it won't drip back onto the granola while it cooks.

6. Cover and cook on low for 6 hours.

7. Transfer the granola to a baking sheet to cool. Store in an airtight container at room temperature or in the refrigerator for up to 2 weeks. You can also freeze the granola for up to 2 months and defrost. Just be sure to wipe off the condensation on the container lid or you'll end up with soggy granola.

vegetable frittata

SERVES 8 TO 12 / COOK TIME: 8 TO 9 HOURS ON LOW

GLUTEN-FREE • VEGETARIAN • PALEO • DAIRY-FREE

Frittatas are probably the easiest breakfast item you can prepare in a slow cooker. There's really no wrong way to make it. I like to think of frittatas as "clean out your produce drawer" meals, because most veggies you find in there are okay to use. This is a great breakfast recipe to prep the evening before and then let it cook overnight.

2 red or green bell peppers, seeded and diced

1 medium onion, diced

½ cup diced tomatoes

1 small zucchini, diced

8 ounces sweet potato, peeled and shredded (optional)

Handful fresh parsley leaves

12 large eggs

1 cup unsweetened almond milk

1 teaspoon salt

½ teaspoon freshly ground black pepper

. . . .

PER SERVING Calories: 162; Total Fat: 8g; Saturated Fat: 2g; Protein: 11g; Carbohydrates: 11g; Cholesterol: 279mg; Sodium: 559mg; Fiber: 2g; Sugar: 5g

1. Combine the bell peppers, onion, tomatoes, zucchini, sweet potato (if using), and parsley in the slow cooker.

2. In a medium bowl, whisk together the eggs, almond milk, salt, and pepper.

3. Pour the egg mixture over of the vegetables in the slow cooker, ensuring that all the vegetables are coated.

4. Cover and cook on low for 8 or 9 hours, or until the eggs are set.

Tip: This is another recipe whose ingredients you can play around with based on your preferences. Add mushrooms, onions, leeks, spinach, kale . . . the possibilities are endless! If you don't have a programmable slow cooker, however, I wouldn't suggest you cook this overnight unless you know you'll be awake to shut it off when it's done. Otherwise you'll wake up to burnt frittata.

kale and mushroom crustless quiche

SERVES 6 / COOK TIME: 8 TO 9 HOURS ON LOW

GLUTEN-FREE • VEGETARIAN

Quiche makes a fantastic brunch dish. I love a good quiche, so I really wanted to include a recipe for one in this cookbook, but I understand that a lot of people are not looking to eat the crust that comes along with it. Therefore, to keep this version low-carb, this quiche is crustless but still has its characteristic rich flavor.

Cooking spray

6 large eggs

2 tablespoons unsweetened almond milk

2 ounces reduced-fat feta cheese, crumbled

¼ cup grated Parmesan cheese

1½ teaspoons Italian Seasoning (page 100)

4 ounces mushrooms, sliced

2 cups chopped kale

....

PER SERVING Calories: 112; Total Fat: 7g; Saturated Fat: 3g; Protein: 10g; Carbohydrates: 4g; Cholesterol: 191mg; Sodium: 163mg; Fiber: 1g; Sugar: 1g

1. Coat the inside of the slow cooker generously with cooking spray.

2. In a large bowl, whisk together the eggs, almond milk, cheeses, and Italian seasoning. Stir in the mushrooms and kale.

3. Pour the mixture into the slow cooker.

4. Cover and cook on low for 8 to 9 hours, or until the eggs are set.

Tip: If you prefer, you can swap out the kale for spinach. The type of cheese is up to you, too—if you don't like feta, try Cheddar or Swiss.

middle eastern shakshuka

SERVES 2 / COOK TIME: 4 TO 6 HOURS ON LOW, PLUS 10 TO 20 MINUTES ON HIGH

GLUTEN-FREE • VEGETARIAN • PALEO • DAIRY-FREE

Shakshuka is a common dish served throughout the Middle East. Since it contains eggs, it's traditionally served for breakfast, but there's no reason not to eat it any time of the day. In my opinion, shakshuka is all about the sauce. The tomato sauce cooks alone with the vegetables and seasonings for the majority of the cook time, with the eggs added last. These cooking instructions offer guidelines for over-medium eggs. If you prefer your eggs more hardboiled, simply cook them a little longer.

1 (28-ounce) can whole tomatoes

2 green or red bell peppers, seeded and diced

1 small onion, diced

4 garlic cloves, minced

Handful fresh parsley leaves

1 teaspoon ground cumin

1 teaspoon salt

½ teaspoon freshly ground black pepper

½ teaspoon ground coriander

½ teaspoon paprika

4 large eggs

....

PER SERVING Calories: 238; Total Fat: 11g; Saturated Fat: 3g; Protein: 19g; Carbohydrates: 29g; Cholesterol: 372mg; Sodium: 1,339mg; Fiber: 9g; Sugar: 16g

1. Combine the tomatoes with their juice, bell peppers, onion, garlic, parsley, cumin, salt, pepper, coriander, and paprika in the slow cooker and mix well.

2. Cover and cook on low for 4 to 6 hours.

3. Make 4 shallow wells in the shakshuka sauce.

4. Crack one egg into each hole.

5. Cover and cook on high for 10 to 20 minutes, or until the eggs are done to your liking. Serve immediately.

Tip: My 4-quart cooker fits the sauce and 4 eggs perfectly. Depending on the size of your slow cooker, you can cut this recipe in half or double it. Shakshuka is made for scooping. For serving, you have several options, depending your dietary needs: your preferred variety of bread—pita works great—or cut-up vegetables like cucumber or celery.

bacon, cheese, and broccoli quiche

SERVES 6 / COOK TIME: 1 TO 2 HOURS ON HIGH, PLUS 6 TO 8 HOURS ON LOW

Though I don't eat it nearly as often as I'd like, quiche is probably my favorite dish for breakfast. I already included Kale and Mushroom Crustless Quiche (page 20), but I love quiche so much, I had to include a traditional version as well. The type of pie crust you choose to use is entirely up to you. The simplest option is a premade refrigerated pie crust (preferably whole wheat); of course, making your own is always a good idea.

Cooking spray

1 (15-ounce) package refrigerated pie crusts (2 rounds)

8 large eggs

1 cup full-fat coconut milk

1 garlic clove, minced

½ teaspoon salt

½ teaspoon freshly ground black pepper

1 cup chopped cooked bacon

½ cup broccoli florets

2 cups shredded low-fat Cheddar cheese

. . . .

PER SERVING Calories: 377; Total Fat: 28g; Saturated Fat: 12g; Protein: 26g; Carbohydrates: 8g; Cholesterol: 300mg; Sodium: 1,135mg; Fiber: 0g; Sugar: 1g

Tip: I recommend using parchment paper under the crust if you have it, because when the quiche has finished cooking, you'll be able to lift it out of the slow cooker by the edges of the paper.

1. Coat the slow cooker generously with cooking spray or line the bottom with parchment paper.

2. Press the pie crusts down in the bottom of the slow cooker and 1 or 2 inches up the sides, overlapping them to make one continuous pie crust.

3. Lay a dish towel or 2 sheets of paper towel between the slow cooker and the lid. This will absorb all the condensation so it won't drip back on the crust while it cooks.

4. Cover and cook on high for 1 to 2 hours.

5. In a medium bowl, whisk together the eggs, coconut milk, garlic, salt, and pepper. Stir in the bacon, broccoli, and cheese. Pour the mixture into the slow cooker.

6. Cover and cook on low for 6 to 8 hours, or until the center of the quiche is set and the edges of the crust are browned. Cool for 10 minutes, then cut and serve.

denver omelet

SERVES 3 / COOK TIME: 4 TO 6 HOURS ON LOW

GLUTEN-FREE

Denver omelets take me back to my childhood. After church every Sunday we would go to Bob Evans, and I would order a Denver omelet with a side of wheat toast. It's no surprise that when I bought my first slow cooker, a Denver omelet was the first recipe I made. This dish always manages to please. If you have a programmable slow cooker, this is a recipe that can be cooked overnight so you wake up to an irresistible-smelling kitchen.

Cooking spray

6 large eggs

1 tablespoon unsweetened almond milk

1 garlic clove, minced

½ teaspoon salt

¼ teaspoon freshly ground black pepper

8 ounces ham, diced

2 red or green bell peppers, seeded and diced

1 small onion, diced

¼ cup diced tomatoes

2 cups shredded low-fat Cheddar cheese, divided

....

PER SERVING Calories: 518; Total Fat: 33g; Saturated Fat: 15g; Protein: 45g; Carbohydrates: 14g; Cholesterol: 468mg; Sodium: 2,140mg; Fiber: 3g; Sugar: 4g

1. Coat the slow cooker generously with cooking spray.

2. In a large bowl, whisk together the eggs, almond milk, garlic, salt, and pepper.

3. Fold in the ham, bell peppers, onion, tomatoes, and 1 cup of shredded cheese.

4. Pour the egg mixture into the slow cooker.

5. Cover and cook on low for 4 to 6 hours, or until the eggs are set.

6. Sprinkle with the remaining 1 cup of shredded cheese before serving.

Tip: If you don't like ham, you can substitute bacon or even turkey bacon. Choose ingredients that fit your lifestyle: If you're vegetarian, omit the meat entirely and load up on your favorite vegetables.

paleo sweet potato hash

SERVES 6 / COOK TIME: 6 TO 8 HOURS ON LOW

GLUTEN-FREE • VEGETARIAN • PALEO • DAIRY-FREE

Paleo is probably the diet I follow most frequently. This recipe represents the epitome of a Paleo breakfast at its most flavorful: eggs, fresh herbs, and sweet potatoes. The homemade hash browns are easy to make and don't add much additional prep time.

Cooking spray

2 pounds sweet potatoes, peeled and shredded

1 small onion, diced

1 green or red bell pepper, diced

12 large eggs

¼ cup unsweetened almond milk

½ teaspoon salt

¼ teaspoon freshly ground black pepper

Chopped fresh herbs, for garnish (optional)

....

PER SERVING Calories: 336; Total Fat: 11g; Saturated Fat: 3g; Protein: 15g; Carbohydrates: 46g; Cholesterol: 372mg; Sodium: 363mg; Fiber: 7g; Sugar: 3g

1. Coat the slow cooker generously with cooking spray.

2. In a medium bowl, toss together the sweet potatoes, onion, and bell pepper.

3. Press the sweet potato mixture into the bottom of the slow cooker. In a large bowl, whisk together the eggs, almond milk, salt, and pepper.

4. Pour the egg mixture into the slow cooker, ensuring that all the sweet potatoes are coated.

5. Cover and cook on low for 6 to 8 hours.

6. Top with fresh herbs, if using, before serving.

Tip: Like the Vegetable Frittata (page 19), this is another recipe you can use to unload your produce drawer— simply add as many vegetables as you like. That's one of the beauties of Paleo eating: unlimited vegetables. You can also add cooked bacon or ground meat.

old-fashioned breakfast casserole

SERVES 8 / COOK TIME: 6 TO 8 HOURS ON LOW

GLUTEN-FREE

We all need a go-to breakfast recipe we know our friends and family can enjoy regardless of dietary restrictions. For me, this is that recipe. When I'm hosting brunch, I like to serve a meal that covers as many bases as possible—this tried-and-true dish includes all the components of a breakfast casserole: eggs, hash browns, meat, cheese, vegetables.

¾ pound ground turkey sausage or bacon

Cooking spray

¾ (28-ounce) bag frozen Potatoes O'Brien or hash browns, thawed

1 cup chopped mushrooms

2 cups shredded Cheddar cheese

12 large eggs

¼ cup unsweetened almond milk

½ teaspoon salt

¼ teaspoon freshly ground black pepper

PER SERVING Calories: 599; Total Fat: 38g; Saturated Fat: 15g; Protein: 24g; Carbohydrates: 39g; Cholesterol: 330mg; Sodium: 834mg; Fiber: 5g; Sugar: 1g

Brown: In a large skillet, brown the ground turkey sausage over medium heat. Drain off the grease.

1. Coat the slow cooker generously with cooking spray.

2. Spread out some of the potatoes in a single layer in the bottom of the slow cooker.

3. Top the potatoes with some of the browned meat, mushrooms, and cheese.

4. Repeat these layers until all the ingredients have been used.

5. In a medium bowl, whisk together the eggs, almond milk, salt, and pepper.

6. Pour the egg mixture on top of the potatoes, meat, and cheese layers, making sure the egg mixture coats all the ingredients.

7. Cover and cook on low for 6 to 8 hours.

Tip: You can vary this recipe as you like. If you don't eat dairy, just omit the cheese. Don't eat meat? Leave it out, and double up on the vegetables. Feel free to substitute your favorite veggies, too—onions, bell peppers, whatever you like.

apple-cinnamon oatmeal

SERVES 4 / COOK TIME: 7 TO 9 HOURS ON LOW

GLUTEN-FREE • VEGETARIAN • DAIRY-FREE

Oatmeal is the perfect overnight slow cooker breakfast. Nutrition-packed steel-cut oats in particular are absolutely made for the low-and-slow method. I eat oatmeal year-round but find it especially comforting during the winter. Something about the sweet aroma of apples and cinnamon makes me dream of cozy mornings in a nice warm kitchen.

Cooking spray

1 apple, cored, peeled, and diced

1 cup steel-cut oats

2½ cups unsweetened vanilla
    almond milk

2 tablespoons honey or maple syrup

½ teaspoon vanilla extract

1 teaspoon ground cinnamon

....

PER SERVING Calories: 126; Total Fat: 3g;
Saturated Fat: 0g; Protein: 3g;
Carbohydrates: 25g; Cholesterol: 0mg;
Sodium: 95mg; Fiber: 4g; Sugar: 15g

1. Coat the slow cooker generously with cooking spray.

2. Combine all the ingredients in the slow cooker and mix well.

3. Cover and cook on low for 7 to 9 hours.

Tip: Spraying your slow cooker beforehand is a must, because oatmeal will stick and is really tough to clean off. Whether you serve it hot or cold is totally up to you. Hot, of course, is the most common way—delicious right out of the slow cooker—but it's also good cold with your preferred milk.

banana-nut oatmeal

SERVES 4 / COOK TIME: 7 TO 9 HOURS ON LOW

GLUTEN-FREE • VEGETARIAN • DAIRY-FREE

Banana-nut is another winning oatmeal pairing. It's probably my favorite oatmeal flavoring next to apple-cinnamon. Bananas offer a wonderful natural sweetness and richness of flavor, all while providing important nutrients like potassium and magnesium. This recipe features steel-cut oats—when it comes to oatmeal, this variety is truly tailor-made for the slow cooker.

Cooking spray

1 cup steel-cut oats

1 ripe banana, mashed

2 cups unsweetened almond milk

1 cup water

1½ tablespoons honey or maple syrup

½ teaspoon vanilla extract

¼ cup chopped almonds, pecans, or walnuts

1 teaspoon ground cinnamon

¼ teaspoon ground nutmeg

....

PER SERVING Calories: 230; Total Fat: 7g; Saturated Fat: 1g; Protein: 5g; Carbohydrates: 40g; Cholesterol: 0mg; Sodium: 94mg; Fiber: 4g; Sugar: 28g

1. Coat the slow cooker generously with cooking spray.

2. Combine all the ingredients in the slow cooker and mix well.

3. Cover and cook on low for 7 to 9 hours.

Tip: Save those brown bananas! The riper, the better in this case, because the riper they get, the sweeter they will be. Depending on the sweetness of the bananas, you may want to adjust the amount of honey.

creamy breakfast quinoa

SERVES 4 / COOK TIME: 7 TO 9 ON HOURS ON LOW

GLUTEN-FREE • VEGETARIAN • DAIRY-FREE

Most people don't realize that quinoa can be eaten for breakfast, but it makes a great protein-filled food to start the day. The fact is it's not much different than oatmeal. It's prepared in a similar manner and you can dress it up like oatmeal as well. This version uses coconut milk to add a creamy texture. If it's too thick, just add water or almond milk until it reaches the consistency of your liking.

1 cup quinoa, rinsed and drained

1½ cups water

1 cup full-fat coconut milk

2 tablespoons honey or maple syrup

½ teaspoon vanilla extract

½ teaspoon ground cinnamon

¼ cup sliced strawberries or other berries, for serving

1. Combine all the ingredients in the slow cooker and mix well.

2. Cover and cook on low for 7 to 9 hours.

3. Top with the berries before serving.

Tip: Quinoa requires a good rinse before cooking to remove the saponins in the grains' coating that make quinoa bitter.

PER SERVING Calories: 224; Total Fat: 6g; Saturated Fat: 3g; Protein: 6g; Carbohydrates: 38g; Cholesterol: 0mg; Sodium: 7mg; Fiber: 3g; Sugar: 10g

dublin coddle

SERVES 6 / COOK TIME: 4 TO 6 HOURS ON LOW

GLUTEN-FREE • PALEO • DAIRY-FREE

I serve this dish every year for St. Patrick's Day breakfast. It's a hearty, Irish slow cooker meal that uses only a few simple, unprocessed ingredients. My version of this traditional dish can be eaten anytime of day, but I like it for breakfast since it includes both sausage and bacon.

¾ pound bacon, cut into 1-inch pieces

¾ pound sausage

1 pound sweet potatoes, peeled and cut into large chunks

2 onions, cut into large chunks

2 garlic cloves, minced

½ teaspoon salt

¼ teaspoon freshly ground black pepper

½ cup low-sodium beef broth

¼ cup chopped fresh parsley, for garnish

. . . .

PER SERVING Calories: 539; Total Fat: 40g; Saturated Fat: 14g; Protein: 17g; Carbohydrates: 26g; Cholesterol: 82mg; Sodium: 1,031mg; Fiber: 4g; Sugar: 2g

Precook: In a large skillet, cook the bacon over medium heat until crisp. Transfer to a paper towel–lined plate. Drain off the grease from the skillet and add the sausage. Cook until browned. Drain off the grease.

1. Spread one-quarter of the sweet potatoes in the slow cooker, then one-quarter of the onions, one-quarter of the bacon, and one-quarter of the sausage. Repeat the layers until all the ingredients are used.

2. Scatter the garlic over the top and season with the salt and pepper.

3. Pour the broth over all the ingredients.

4. Cover and cook on low for 4 to 6 hours.

5. Garnish with the parsley before serving.

Tip: For a more complete breakfast, pair this recipe with an egg or two cooked in your favorite style. You can also substitute any form of potato for the sweet potatoes—whatever best suits your dietary needs.

Indian-Spiced Chicken Stew *page 41*

soups, stews, curries, and chilies

simple tomato soup

SERVES 4 / COOK TIME: 6 TO 8 HOURS ON LOW

GLUTEN-FREE • VEGAN • PALEO • DAIRY-FREE

This tomato soup is a classic for a reason, and it couldn't get any easier. Just throw everything in the slow cooker and let it cook. I make numerous batches of this whenever someone feels under the weather. I even made it twice in one day this past fall!

2 pounds Roma tomatoes, sliced

3 garlic heads, cloves peeled

1 onion, chopped

2 cups low-sodium vegetable broth

1 teaspoon extra-virgin olive oil

1 teaspoon salt, plus extra for seasoning

¼ teaspoon freshly ground black pepper, plus extra for seasoning

....

PER SERVING Calories: 110; Total Fat: 2g; Saturated Fat: 0g; Protein: 5g; Carbohydrates: 18g; Cholesterol: 0mg; Sodium: 632mg; Fiber: 4g; Sugar: 7g

1. Combine all the ingredients in the slow cooker and mix well.

2. Cover and cook on low for 6 to 8 hours.

3. Pour the contents of the slow cooker into a blender or food processor and blend until smooth. (If using a blender, remove the center cap from the blender lid and hold a dish towel firmly over the hole while blending to allow the steam to escape.)

4. Taste and season with additional salt and pepper if needed.

Tip: No need to peel the tomatoes first—they go in raw with their skins still on. But if you have time to roast the tomatoes, garlic, and onion beforehand, I highly recommend you do so. The char on the veggies will add a nice roasted flavor to the soup.

unstuffed cabbage roll soup

SERVES 4 / COOK TIME: 6 TO 8 HOURS ON LOW

GLUTEN-FREE • PALEO • DAIRY-FREE

This is a great recipe to use up that leftover brown rice (or quinoa) you have in the refrigerator. Or, if you're on a low-carb diet, you can substitute 1 cup of cauliflower rice. Put the cauliflower rice in raw—don't worry, it won't turn to mush.

1¼ pounds extra-lean ground beef

1 medium yellow onion, chopped

4 garlic cloves, minced

4 green cabbage heads, cored and chopped

1 (32-ounce) carton low-sodium beef broth

2 cups tomato sauce

1 teaspoon salt

1 teaspoon dried parsley

½ teaspoon dried oregano

½ teaspoon freshly ground black pepper

1 cup cooked brown rice, for serving

1. Combine all the ingredients in the slow cooker and mix well.

2. Cover and cook on low for 6 to 8 hours.

3. Stir in the brown rice before serving.

Tip: You might not guess it, but this makes a great freezer meal. Simply combine all the ingredients except the beef broth in a resealable plastic bag and freeze. When ready to cook, defrost the bag overnight in the refrigerator, then transfer everything to the slow cooker, along with the broth.

PER SERVING Calories: 587; Total Fat: 17g; Saturated Fat: 1g; Protein: 50g; Carbohydrates: 64g; Cholesterol: 0mg; Sodium: 2,077mg; Fiber: 21g; Sugar: 30g

paleo butternut squash soup

SERVES 4 / COOK TIME: 6 TO 8 HOURS ON LOW

GLUTEN-FREE • PALEO • VEGAN • DAIRY-FREE

My friend makes the best butternut squash soup every year for Thanksgiving, so when he finally shared his recipe with me, I reworked it to make it Paleo. I simply substituted full-fat coconut milk for the heavy cream and sweet potatoes for the russets.

2 pounds butternut squash, peeled and diced

1 pound sweet potatoes, peeled and diced

1 celery stalk, chopped

¼ cup chopped fresh cilantro

1 tablespoon curry powder

1 teaspoon salt

1 teaspoon freshly ground black pepper

½ teaspoon ground cumin

¼ teaspoon ground nutmeg

1 (15-ounce) can full-fat coconut milk

....

PER SERVING Calories: 305; Total Fat: 7g; Saturated Fat: 6g; Protein: 5g; Carbohydrates: 61g; Cholesterol: 0g; Sodium: 604g; Fiber: 10g; Sugar: 6g

1. Combine the butternut squash, sweet potatoes, celery, cilantro, curry powder, salt, pepper, cumin, and nutmeg in the slow cooker.

2. Add enough water to cover all the ingredients.

3. Cover and cook on low for 6 to 8 hours, or until the butternut squash and sweet potatoes are tender.

4. Using a blender or food processor, blend the soup to your desired consistency. (If using a blender, remove the center cap from the blender lid and hold a dish towel firmly over the hole while blending to allow the steam to escape.)

5. Stir in the coconut milk before serving.

> **Tip:** I like to top each bowl of this soup with a few crumbles of cooked bacon. While this is optional, I'd definitely recommend it, if your diet allows.

tex-mex chicken soup

SERVES 6 / COOK TIME: 6 TO 8 HOURS ON LOW

GLUTEN-FREE • DAIRY-FREE

Tex-Mex is the term used to describe a fusion of Texan and Mexican cuisines. Most of the ingredients are common in Mexican dishes, like cilantro and corn. This recipe uses boneless, skinless chicken thighs. You can use white meat like chicken breasts. If you do, reduce the cook time by 1–2 hours. If you already have cooked meat on hand, you can certainly use that, too!

2 pounds boneless, skinless chicken thighs

1 (28-ounce) can crushed tomatoes

1 (15-ounce) can corn, drained

Handful chopped fresh cilantro

1 teaspoon chili powder

1 teaspoon ground cumin

1 teaspoon dried oregano

1 teaspoon salt

½ teaspoon freshly ground black pepper

1 avocado, sliced (optional)

....

PER SERVING Calories: 334; Total Fat: 13g; Saturated Fat: 3g; Protein: 35g; Carbohydrates: 22g; Cholesterol: 127mg; Sodium: 913mg; Fiber: 8g; Sugar: 9g

1. Combine all the ingredients except the avocado in the slow cooker and mix well.

2. Cover and cook on low for 6 to 8 hours.

3. Top each serving with a couple slices of avocado, if using.

Tip: A great way to cut back on your sodium intake is to use dried beans rather than canned. Dried beans contain less sodium and are usually cheaper, too. Soak them overnight before using.

stuffed pepper soup

SERVES 4 / COOK TIME: 6 TO 8 HOURS ON LOW

GLUTEN-FREE • DAIRY-FREE

As much as I love stuffed peppers, I love stuffed pepper soup even more. It's the best of both worlds—the heartiness of stuffed bell peppers along with the comfort of a slow-cooked soup. Feel free to substitute cauliflower rice for brown rice if you're following a low-carb diet.

1½ pounds extra-lean ground beef

1 medium onion, diced

1 (15-ounce) can diced tomatoes, with their juice

1 (15-ounce) can tomato sauce

2 green or red bell peppers, seeded and diced

2 cups low-sodium beef broth

1 cup cooked brown rice

1. Combine all the ingredients in the slow cooker and mix well.

2. Cover and cook on low for 6 to 8 hours.

Tip: To save you the time of browning the meat, this recipe calls for adding the meat to the soup raw. To minimize the amount of grease in the soup, use the leanest ground beef you can find.

PER SERVING Calories: 337; Total Fat: 8g; Saturated Fat: 3g; Protein: 41g; Carbohydrates: 27g; Cholesterol: 90mg; Sodium: 432mg; Fiber: 5g; Sugar: 11g

pepperoni pizza soup

SERVES 4 / COOK TIME: 6 TO 8 HOURS ON LOW

GLUTEN-FREE • PALEO • DAIRY-FREE

This recipe is so versatile—using different combinations of meats and veggies will create endless variations. For example, you might try ground turkey, turkey pepperoni, and low-sodium chicken broth instead of the ground beef, regular pepperoni, and beef broth. This is a kid-friendly recipe the entire family will enjoy.

1 pound extra-lean ground beef

¼ cup chopped pepperoni

1 small onion, chopped

4 ounces mushrooms, sliced

1 (32-ounce) carton low-sodium beef broth

1 (15-ounce) can tomato sauce

1 (15-ounce) can diced tomatoes, with their juice

1 (4-ounce) can diced green chiles, drained

1 (2½-ounce) can sliced black olives, drained

2 tablespoons dried oregano

1 tablespoon dried basil

1 teaspoon salt

¼ cup shredded mozzarella cheese, for topping (optional)

1. Combine all the ingredients in the slow cooker and mix well.
2. Cover and cook on low for 6 to 8 hours.
3. If desired, top with the cheese before serving.

Tip: If you have the time, brown the ground beef so you can drain the grease before adding the meat to the slow cooker.

PER SERVING Calories: 312; Total Fat: 13g; Saturated Fat: 5g; Protein: 33g; Carbohydrates: 17g; Cholesterol: 77mg; Sodium: 1,551mg; Fiber: 5g; Sugar: 10g

pot roast soup

SERVES 6 / COOK TIME: 6 TO 8 HOURS ON LOW

GLUTEN-FREE • PALEO • DAIRY-FREE

This is really a reworking of my classic slow cooker roast recipe. It occurred to me one day: roast and soup, two things I love. Why not combine them? Like a roast, this soup will have your whole kitchen smelling amazing! And as with a slow cooker roast, you'll know the beef is done when the meat is so tender it's falling apart.

2 pounds beef stew meat

2 (32-ounce) cartons low-sodium beef broth

1½ pounds sweet potatoes, peeled and chopped

3 carrots, peeled and chopped

3 celery stalks, chopped

1 medium onion, chopped

½ teaspoon paprika

½ teaspoon ground cumin

½ teaspoon onion powder

½ teaspoon garlic powder

½ teaspoon dried oregano

½ teaspoon salt

½ teaspoon freshly ground black pepper

1. Combine all the ingredients in the slow cooker and mix well.

2. Cover and cook on low for 6 to 8 hours.

Tip: As with most roasts, this soup is even better the next day. Sometimes I double the recipe to guarantee that I'll have leftovers.

PER SERVING Calories: 444; Total Fat: 10g; Saturated Fat: 4g; Protein: 48g; Carbohydrates: 34g; Cholesterol: 135mg; Sodium: 412mg; Fiber: 6g; Sugar: 3g

paleo pumpkin bisque

SERVES 6 / COOK TIME: 6 TO 8 HOURS ON LOW

GLUTEN-FREE • PALEO

Most people tend to cook with pumpkin only during autumn. This recipe, however, is meant to be shared year-round. I know it's hard to get your hands on fresh pumpkin in the spring or summer, so canned pumpkin is okay to use. Just be sure to check the ingredients label. If only one ingredient—pumpkin—is listed, then use it. This version is Paleo, so it uses coconut milk.

4 slices bacon, cooked and crumbled

1 (15-ounce) can pure pumpkin

1 (15-ounce) can full-fat coconut milk

1 cup low-sodium chicken or
   vegetable broth

1 small onion, cut into quarters

3 garlic cloves, minced

1 (1-inch) piece ginger, peeled

1 teaspoon ghee

1 teaspoon pumpkin pie spice

1 teaspoon salt

½ teaspoon ground cinnamon

. . . .

PER SERVING Calories: 387; Total Fat: 34g; Saturated Fat: 25g; Protein: 9g; Carbohydrates: 14g; Cholesterol: 16mg; Sodium: 456mg; Fiber: 3g; Sugar: 6g

1. Combine half of the crumbled bacon and all the remaining ingredients in the slow cooker and mix well.

2. Cover and cook on low for 6 to 8 hours.

3. Remove and discard the ginger.

4. Using a countertop blender or immersion blender, process until smooth. (If using a countertop blender, remove the center cap from the blender lid and hold a dish towel firmly over the hole while blending to allow the steam to escape.)

5. Top with the remaining crumbled bacon before serving.

Tip: Using full-fat coconut milk results in a creamy bisque. For a less creamy version, try to find light coconut milk. It's a little harder to locate and can be a tad more expensive, so if it's not available, use full-fat and add a teaspoon or so of water.

split pea soup with smoked turkey

SERVES 6 / COOK TIME: 10 TO 12 HOURS ON LOW

GLUTEN-FREE • DAIRY-FREE

This isn't your usual split pea soup, due to the lack of a ham bone. In fact, there's no ham of any kind. If you don't eat pork, smoked turkey provides a good substitute for the ham—its smokiness gives the turkey a similar flavor. This is hands-down one of the easiest soups you can make in your slow cooker. It uses only a few simple ingredients, mainly green split peas, celery carrots, onion, and smoked turkey.

1 pound green split peas, soaked overnight and drained

1 pound smoked turkey, shredded or chopped

2 celery stalks, chopped

2 medium carrots, peeled and chopped

1 onion, chopped

2 garlic cloves, minced

1 teaspoon salt

1 teaspoon freshly ground black pepper

1. Combine all the ingredients in the slow cooker.

2. Add enough water to cover all the ingredients.

3. Cover and cook on low for 10 to 12 hours, stirring occasionally.

4. Add more water if the consistency is too thick for your liking.

PER SERVING Calories: 437; Total Fat: 2g; Saturated Fat: 0g; Protein: 54g; Carbohydrates: 53g; Cholesterol: 67mg; Sodium: 1,392mg; Fiber: 20g; Sugar: 8g

Tip: This soup cooks for 10 to 12 hours. This is a great recipe to prepare overnight or even the day before you want to serve it. The consistency will thicken after it sits and cools, so add water if you prefer it thinner. You can also use Beef or Chicken Bone Broth (page 13) instead of water if you like.

indian-spiced chicken stew

SERVES 4 / COOK TIME: 5 TO 7 HOURS ON LOW

GLUTEN-FREE • DAIRY-FREE

I love Indian food. You'll find a lot of Indian recipes in this cookbook, and this one in particular is close to my heart. In fact, it's one of the first recipes I created when I started my food blog. This dish does not have the usual thickness of a traditional Indian curry—its consistency is more of a soup or stew. If you prefer a more conventional curry texture, whisk together ¼ cup of water and 2 tablespoons of arrowroot powder, and stir this into the stew during the last 30 minutes.

2 to 3 pounds boneless, skinless chicken thighs, cut into bite-size pieces

2 cups low-sodium chicken broth

1 pound red potatoes, diced

1 onion, chopped

3 garlic cloves, minced

1 (8-ounce) can tomato sauce

2 teaspoons garam masala

2 teaspoons ground cumin

2 teaspoons ground ginger

2 teaspoons ground turmeric

1 teaspoon ground coriander

½ teaspoon cayenne pepper

Cilantro, for garnish (optional)

1. Combine all the ingredients in the slow cooker and mix well.
2. Cover and cook on low for 5 to 7 hours. Serve garnished with cilantro, if desired.

Tip: If you can't find garam masala, just substitute curry powder.

PER SERVING Calories: 379; Total Fat: 10g; Saturated Fat: 2g; Protein: 48g; Carbohydrates: 25g; Cholesterol: 189mg; Sodium: 407mg; Fiber: 4g; Sugar: 4g

paleo chicken and butternut squash stew

SERVES 4 / COOKING TIME: 5 TO 7 HOURS ON LOW

GLUTEN-FREE • PALEO

Many supermarkets sell butternut squash already cut up in the produce department, which can save you even more prep time! If you can't find butternut squash, just look for acorn or pumpkin.

2 pounds boneless, skinless chicken thighs, cut into bite-size pieces

1 medium onion, sliced

2 pounds butternut squash, peeled, seeded, and cubed

1 (15-ounce) can coconut cream or full-fat coconut milk

1 teaspoon ghee

1½ teaspoons poultry seasoning

1 teaspoon salt

¼ teaspoon freshly ground black pepper

¼ teaspoon ground nutmeg

Handful chopped fresh rosemary leaves (optional)

1. Combine the chicken, onion, and butternut squash in the slow cooker.

2. In a small bowl, combine the coconut cream, ghee, poultry seasoning, salt, pepper, nutmeg, and rosemary (if using).

3. Pour the sauce into the slow cooker, and stir to make sure the chicken, onion, and squash are well coated.

4. Cover and cook on low for 5 to 7 hours.

Tip: I recommend using chicken thighs for the slow cooker. Chicken breasts taste great, but you run the risk of over-cooking them, as white meat generally cooks a bit faster than dark meat.

PER SERVING Calories: 521; Total Fat: 24g; Saturated Fat: 16g; Protein: 48g; Carbohydrates: 32g; Cholesterol: 192mg; Sodium: 803mg; Fiber: 5g; Sugar: 6g

hamburger stew

SERVES 4 / COOK TIME: 6 TO 8 HOURS ON LOW

GLUTEN-FREE • PALEO • DAIRY-FREE

Hamburger flavors in a soup! Not just any soup, a healthy Paleo soup that provides comfort without the calories. Use your preferred ground meat, whether it's beef, pork, chicken, or turkey, though I think ground beef works best. If potatoes or sweet potatoes aren't on your diet, simply omit them from the recipe.

2 pounds extra-lean ground beef

1 pound sweet potatoes, peeled and chopped, or red potatoes, chopped

1 (28-ounce) can diced tomatoes, with their juice

1 (15-ounce) can diced tomatoes, with their juice

1 onion, chopped

1 red or green bell pepper, seeded and chopped

2 celery stalks, chopped

2 garlic cloves, minced

Handful chopped fresh parsley

1½ teaspoons ground mustard

1 teaspoon garlic powder

1 teaspoon salt

½ teaspoon freshly ground black pepper

1. Combine all the ingredients in the slow cooker and mix well.

2. Cover and cook on low for 6 to 8 hours.

Tip: If you prefer to make this more of a soup than a stew, add 2 cups of Beef or Chicken Bone Broth (page 13).

PER SERVING Calories: 472; Total Fat: 11g; Saturated Fat: 4g; Protein: 56g; Carbohydrates: 38g; Cholesterol: 119mg; Sodium: 781mg; Fiber: 10g; Sugar: 11g

lentil and tomato stew

SERVES 4 / COOK TIME: 6 TO 8 HOURS ON LOW

GLUTEN-FREE • VEGAN • DAIRY-FREE

Shop at Trader Joe's, anyone? Have you tasted their one-minute lentil salad? My friend served it for dinner (sans the feta), and I was immediately hooked. This recipe is essentially lentils, tomatoes, broth, and a few seasonings—that's it. Lentils are naturally gluten-free and packed with protein and fiber, plus they're fat-free and low-calorie to boot.

2 pounds Roma tomatoes, diced

1 cup lentils, rinsed and drained

1 (32-ounce) carton low-sodium vegetable broth

¼ cup chopped fresh basil

1 tablespoon balsamic vinegar

4 garlic cloves, minced

1 teaspoon salt

½ teaspoon freshly ground black pepper

1. Combine all the ingredients in the slow cooker and mix well.

2. Cover and cook on low for 6 to 8 hours, or until the lentils are tender.

Tip: You can eat this straight out of the bowl or, if your diet permits, sop up the stew's tasty broth with a slice of bread.

PER SERVING Calories: 119; Total Fat: 1g; Saturated Fat: 0g; Protein: 9g; Carbohydrates: 21g; Cholesterol: 0mg; Sodium: 660mg; Fiber: 7g; Sugar: 7g

all-american beef stew

SERVES 4 / COOK TIME: 8 TO 9 HOURS ON LOW

GLUTEN-FREE • PALEO • DAIRY-FREE

I couldn't write a slow cooker cookbook without including a recipe for beef stew. Traditional, old-fashioned, classic—whatever you want to call it, beef stew is a staple in households across America. And rightfully so. It's a dish almost impossible to mess up. And depending on which ingredients you choose add, you can make the stew as healthy as you like. This recipe keeps it simple—how you embellish it from here is up to you.

2 pounds beef stew meat

1 pound sweet potatoes, peeled and chopped

3 medium carrots, peeled and chopped

1 medium onion, chopped

2 celery stalks, chopped

1 teaspoon salt

½ teaspoon freshly ground black pepper

1 (32-ounce) carton low-sodium beef broth

1. Combine the meat, sweet potatoes, carrots, onion, celery, salt, and pepper in the slow cooker.

2. Pour the broth over the top.

3. Cover and cook on low for 8 to 9 hours.

Tip: Since this recipe requires a lot of broth, it's best to use one that is low-sodium. I'd suggest fat-free broth as well. And if time allows, brown the meat before adding it to the slow cooker.

PER SERVING Calories: 499; Total Fat: 12g; Saturated Fat: 4g; Protein: 52g; Carbohydrates: 39g; Cholesterol: 149mg; Sodium: 621mg; Fiber: 7g; Sugar: 4g

vegan indian curry
with chickpeas and vegetables

SERVES 4 / COOK TIME: 6 TO 8 HOURS ON LOW

GLUTEN-FREE • VEGAN • DAIRY-FREE

I try to eat vegetarian at least once a week and find Indian recipes to be great for vegetarian or even vegan meals. While I used sweet potatoes in this recipe, you can certainly substitute the white potatoes normally used in curries. Waxy potatoes like red potatoes are best because they hold their shape better then starchy ones. If you find that your curry comes out a bit too dry, try adding more coconut milk or even water.

1 (15-ounce) can chickpeas, rinsed and drained

½ cup light coconut milk

2 medium sweet potatoes, peeled and diced

1 medium onion, diced

2 garlic cloves, minced

1 tablespoon curry powder

1½ teaspoons ground ginger

1 teaspoon ground cumin

1 teaspoon ground turmeric

1 teaspoon ground coriander

1 teaspoon red pepper flakes

½ cup frozen peas

1 cup cherry tomatoes, halved

1. Combine the chickpeas, coconut milk, sweet potatoes, onion, garlic, and seasonings in the slow cooker and mix well.

2. Cover and cook on low for 6 to 8 hours.

3. During the last 30 minutes of cook time, add the peas and tomatoes. Stir to mix well, re-cover, and finish cooking.

Tip: I know one of the best things about slow cooker meals is the set-it-and-forget-it factor. If you don't think you'll have time to add the peas and tomatoes during the last 30 minutes of cook time, just include them with the rest of the ingredients at the beginning.

PER SERVING Calories: 223; Total Fat: 3g; Saturated Fat: 2g; Protein: 7g; Carbohydrates: 44g; Cholesterol: 0mg; Sodium: 150mg; Fiber: 7g; Sugar: 7g

spicy sweet potato curry

SERVES 4 / COOK TIME: 6 TO 8 HOURS ON LOW

GLUTEN-FREE • VEGAN • DAIRY-FREE

I would describe this vegan curry as Indian with hints of Thai. For me, the hard part was deciding how to serve it. Over brown basmati rice? Or quinoa? With naan? All delicious options. And sometimes I serve it in warm tortillas!

1 pound sweet potatoes, peeled and chopped

1 onion, chopped

2 carrots, peeled and chopped

1 (15-ounce) can chickpeas, rinsed and drained

1 (15-ounce) can light coconut milk

1 cup water

1 cup frozen green peas

4 garlic cloves, minced

2 Roma tomatoes, chopped, plus extra for garnish

2 teaspoons ground cumin

1 teaspoon ground ginger

1 teaspoon ground turmeric

1 teaspoon dried thyme

1 teaspoon salt

1 teaspoon cayenne pepper

Chopped fresh cilantro, for garnish

1. Combine all the ingredients in the slow cooker and mix well.

2. Cover and cook on low for 6 to 8 hours. Garnish with chopped tomatoes and cilantro before serving.

Tip: Sweet potatoes are an excellent source of vitamin A, vitamin C, potassium, and dietary fiber. However, whenever you see sweet potatoes called for in a recipe, feel free to swap them for the potato of your choice.

PER SERVING Calories: 339; Total Fat: 9g; Saturated Fat: 6g; Protein: 9g; Carbohydrates: 59g; Cholesterol: 0mg; Sodium: 778mg; Fiber: 9g; Sugar: 10g

old-fashioned chili

SERVES 6 / COOK TIME: 6 TO 8 HOURS ON LOW

GLUTEN-FREE • DAIRY-FREE

Hands down my favorite thing to prepare in the slow cooker is chili. Yes, I went there. The low-and-slow method both draws out and meshes the flavors of all the tasty ingredients. I always think that chili tastes better the next day, after sitting in the fridge overnight. Everyone has their own chili recipe they think is simply the best. I've been making this one for years, and I think you'll find it has just the right amount of heat.

1 pound ground beef

1 pound ground pork sausage

1 (28-ounce) can crushed tomatoes

1 (10-ounce) can diced tomatoes with green chiles, with their juice

1 (8-ounce) can tomato sauce

1 (15-ounce) can red kidney beans, rinsed and drained

1 onion, chopped

3 garlic cloves, minced

2 tablespoons chili powder

2 teaspoons ground cumin

1½ teaspoons paprika

1 teaspoon dried oregano

1 teaspoon salt

½ teaspoon freshly ground black pepper

Brown: In a large skillet, brown the ground beef and sausage over medium heat. Drain off the grease.

1. Combine all the ingredients, including the browned meats, in the slow cooker and mix well.

2. Cover and cook on low 6 to 8 hours.

Tip: I know prep like browning the meat should be an optional step, but it's important for this chili since the sausage needs it, too. Together the beef and sausage will emit quite a bit of grease, which you will drain before adding the meat to the slow cooker.

PER SERVING Calories: 422; Total Fat: 23g; Saturated Fat: 8g; Protein: 32g; Carbohydrates: 23g; Cholesterol: 94mg; Sodium: 1,456mg; Fiber: 9g; Sugar: 12g

indian chicken chili

SERVES 4 / COOK TIME: 6 TO 8 HOURS ON LOW

GLUTEN-FREE • DAIRY-FREE

This chili uses traditional Indian spices and ingredients for a unique twist on a traditional slow cooker classic. This is another recipe that you can tweak to your liking. For example, I really enjoy bell peppers, so I suggest using two. I also used ground chicken, but you can substitute your preferred meat.

2 pounds ground chicken

1 (15-ounce) can chickpeas

1 (15-ounce) can diced tomatoes, with their juice

1 (8-ounce) can tomato sauce

1 onion, diced

2 red or green bell peppers, seeded and diced

3 garlic cloves, minced

2 tablespoons garam masala or curry powder

2 teaspoons ground cumin

1½ teaspoons salt

½ teaspoon paprika

½ teaspoons dried oregano

1. Combine all the ingredients in the slow cooker and mix well.

2. Cover and cook on low 6 to 8 hours.

Tip: You can use either garam masala or curry powder, but I prefer garam masala for this dish. As with most chilies, this tastes even better the next day.

PER SERVING Calories: 529; Total Fat: 20g; Saturated Fat: 5g; Protein: 48g; Carbohydrates: 41g; Cholesterol: 194mg; Sodium: 3,420mg; Fiber: 9g; Sugar: 9g

chunky beef chili with sweet potatoes

SERVES 4 / COOK TIME: 6 TO 8 HOURS ON LOW

GLUTEN-FREE • PALEO • DAIRY-FREE

I'll repeat this until the cows come home: Slow cookers were made for chili. It is without a doubt the perfect dish to cook in your slow cooker. I love chili because it's almost impossible to make a mistake, and the options are endless for adding your own twists. Make yours vegetarian, packed with meat, using three beans—whatever appeals to you on any given day. Unlike many recipes, this chili does not use any beans. In their place, I chose to load this dish up with sweet potatoes and vegetables.

1 pound ground beef

1 pound beef stew meat

1 pound sweet potatoes, peeled and chopped

2 red or green bell peppers, seeded and chopped

1 large onion, chopped

1 (28-ounce) can whole tomatoes, with their juice

3 garlic cloves, minced

2 tablespoons chili powder

1 tablespoon sea salt

2 teaspoons ground cumin

1 teaspoon paprika

1 teaspoon dried oregano

Brown: In a large skillet, brown the ground beef and stew meat over medium heat. Drain off the grease.

1. Combine all the ingredients, including the browned meats, in the slow cooker and mix well.

2. Cover and cook on low for 6 to 8 hours.

Tip: Browning the meat is an important step in this recipe, at least with the ground beef, since you will need to drain the grease before adding the meat to the slow cooker.

PER SERVING Calories: 466; Total Fat: 16g; Saturated Fat: 5g; Protein: 52g; Carbohydrates: 30g; Cholesterol: 115mg; Sodium: 1,586mg; Fiber: 7g; Sugar: 10g

southwestern black bean chili

SERVES 6 / COOK TIME: 6 TO 8 HOURS ON LOW

GLUTEN-FREE • DAIRY-FREE

I kept this chili recipe simple, so think of it as a base to which you can add your favorite ingredients. It's always a good idea to pile on some vegetables such as bell peppers. For the meat, ground beef, turkey, chicken, or pork all make great options. This recipe uses my homemade Taco Seasoning. You can always use a premade packet if you want, but making your own taco seasoning blend is super-easy and contains half the sodium.

FOR THE CHILI

1 pound lean ground turkey

1 small onion, diced

1 (15-ounce) can black beans, rinsed and drained

1 (15-ounce) can corn, drained

1 (28-ounce) diced tomatoes, with their juice

FOR THE TACO SEASONING

1 tablespoon chili powder

1½ teaspoons ground cumin

1 teaspoon salt

1 teaspoon freshly ground black pepper

½ teaspoon dried oregano

½ teaspoon paprika

¼ teaspoon garlic powder

¼ teaspoon onion powder

¼ teaspoon red pepper flakes

1. Combine all the ingredients in the slow cooker and mix well.

2. Cover and cook on low for 6 to 8 hours.

Tip: This recipe is more versatile than you think: Turn it into a healthy taco soup by adding 2 cups of low-sodium broth. And if you're feeding a larger crowd, just double the recipe.

PER SERVING Calories: 231; Total Fat: 7g; Saturated Fat: 2g; Protein: 21g; Carbohydrates: 24g; Cholesterol: 54mg; Sodium: 528mg; Fiber: 7g; Sugar: 7g

Quinoa Risotto with Turnip and Kale *page 54*

pasta, rice, and other grains

quinoa risotto with turnip and kale

SERVES 4 / COOK TIME: 6 TO 8 HOURS ON LOW

GLUTEN-FREE • VEGAN • PALEO • DAIRY-FREE

Technically this isn't risotto at all—quinoa risotto is pretty much just creamy quinoa. It's the coconut milk that produces the creamy consistency in this case. Use either light or full-fat coconut milk, whichever you prefer. I like to use light in this recipe because of its milder flavor. If you'd rather avoid coconut in general, try adding ¼ cup additional broth instead.

1 cup quinoa, rinsed and drained

1 medium turnip, peeled and chopped

2 garlic cloves, minced

2 cups low-sodium vegetable broth

½ cup light coconut milk

1½ teaspoons ground cumin

1 teaspoon salt

½ teaspoon freshly ground
   black pepper

2 cups chopped kale

Goji berries, for garnish (optional)

. . . .

PER SERVING Calories: 272; Total Fat: 10g; Saturated Fat: 7g; Protein: 10g; Carbohydrates: 37g; Cholesterol: 0mg; Sodium: 663mg; Fiber: 5g; Sugar: 2g

1. Combine the quinoa, turnip, garlic, broth, coconut milk, cumin, salt, and pepper in the slow cooker and mix well.

2. Cover and cook on low for 6 to 8 hours.

3. During the last 30 minutes of cook time, stir in the kale, re-cover, and finish cooking.

4. Top with goji berries (if using).

Tip: Rinse the quinoa thoroughly in a fine-mesh strainer for 30 seconds or so before use to remove the saponins, the natural coating that creates a bitter taste. If you won't be available to add the kale during the last 30 minutes of cook time, just add it at the beginning—it will simply come out very soft.

lemon-pepper chicken and brown rice

SERVES 6 / COOK TIME: 4 TO 6 HOURS ON LOW, PLUS 15 TO 30 MINUTES ON HIGH

GLUTEN-FREE • DAIRY-FREE

For this citrus-infused chicken recipe, my favorite cut to use is drumsticks. To increase the nutritional value, the chicken is paired with brown rice, which contains fiber. Among its many benefits, fiber has been shown to reduce cholesterol levels and help control blood sugar levels, making brown rice an excellent grain choice for diabetics.

2 cups low-sodium chicken broth

¼ cup freshly squeezed lemon juice

1 teaspoon grated lemon zest

2 garlic cloves, minced

1⅛ teaspoons freshly ground black pepper

¼ teaspoon paprika

2 pounds chicken drumsticks

1 lemon, sliced (optional)

2 cups instant brown rice

....

PER SERVING Calories: 518; Total Fat: 21g; Saturated Fat: 6g; Protein: 34g; Carbohydrates: 49g; Cholesterol: 127mg; Sodium: 223mg; Fiber: 2g; Sugar: 0g

1. In a small bowl, whisk together the broth, lemon juice and zest, garlic, pepper, and paprika. Pour the mixture into the bottom of the slow cooker.

2. Add the chicken pieces to the slow cooker. If you are using the lemon slices, add those on top of the chicken.

3. Cover and cook on low for 4 to 6 hours.

4. Stir in the brown rice.

5. Cover and cook on high for 15 to 30 minutes, or until the rice is tender.

Tip: Use instant brown rice in this recipe, not regular brown rice, as the regular variety won't cook in time. You will know the dish is done when all the liquid is absorbed.

cajun chicken with pasta

SERVES 6 / COOK TIME: 4 TO 6 HOURS ON LOW, PLUS 20 TO 30 MINUTES ON HIGH

GLUTEN-FREE • DAIRY-FREE

Please don't confuse Cajun with spicy. This dish is full of Cajun flavor, but it's not packing much heat. If you're looking for a spicier dish, I suggest adding 1 teaspoon of cayenne pepper or chili powder. Use your favorite shape of pasta: penne, fettuccine, linguine, or whatever you like best. Swap in quinoa pasta or brown rice pasta to make this dish gluten-free.

¼ cup water

2 tablespoons arrowroot powder

2 pounds boneless, skinless chicken thighs

1 (28-ounce) can diced tomatoes, with their juice

1 green or red bell pepper, seeded and diced

1 medium red onion, diced

2 garlic cloves, minced

1 tablespoon Cajun seasoning

1 teaspoon dried oregano

½ teaspoon salt

¼ teaspoon freshly ground black pepper

8 ounces whole-wheat pasta, quinoa pasta, or brown rice pasta

1. In a small bowl, whisk together the water and arrowroot.

2. Combine the arrowroot mixture, chicken, tomatoes with their juice, bell pepper, onion, garlic, Cajun seasoning, oregano, salt, and pepper in the slow cooker and mix well.

3. Cover and cook on low for 4 to 6 hours.

4. Add the pasta and stir until completely submerged, with no pieces sticking out.

5. Cover and cook on high for 20 to 30 minutes, or until the pasta is tender.

Tip: One of the keys to cooking pasta in the slow cooker is to make sure there is enough liquid to cover it. You will also need to keep an eye on it and give it an occasional stir.

PER SERVING Calories: 358; Total Fat: 7g; Saturated Fat: 1g; Protein: 36g; Carbohydrates: 36g; Cholesterol: 127mg; Sodium: 336mg; Fiber: 6g; Sugar: 6g

old-school chicken noodle soup

SERVES 4 / COOK TIME: 5 TO 7 HOURS ON LOW, PLUS 20 TO 30 MINUTES ON HIGH

GLUTEN-FREE • DAIRY-FREE

Chicken noodle soup is another must-have recipe for a slow cooker cookbook. A lot of people don't think to make chicken noodle soup in their slow cooker, but to me, it's a perfect match. While noodle soup is eaten around the globe, with different spins in the cuisine of every region, this recipe is for the traditional American version.

1 pound boneless, skinless chicken thighs, cut into bite-size pieces

6 cups low-sodium chicken broth

1 cup water

1 tablespoons extra-virgin olive oil

4 carrots, peeled and chopped

3 celery stalks, chopped

1 onion, diced

4 garlic cloves, minced

2 bay leaves

1 teaspoon celery salt

1 teaspoon dried thyme

1 teaspoon dried rosemary

½ teaspoon salt

½ teaspoon freshly ground black pepper

8 ounces egg noodles, gluten-free if desired

1. Combine the chicken, broth, water, olive oil, carrots, celery, onion, garlic, bay leaves, and seasonings in the slow cooker and mix well.

2. Cover and cook on low for 5 to 7 hours.

3. Remove the bay leaves and discard. Remove the chicken from the slow cooker and shred with two forks.

4. Return the shredded chicken to the slow cooker and add the noodles.

5. Cover and cook on high for 20 to 30 minutes, or until the noodles are tender.

Tip: As with most pasta recipes here, you can use your choice of noodles. For my chicken noodle soup, I tend to use spaghetti, but that's just personal preference.

PER SERVING Calories: 520; Total Fat: 12g; Saturated Fat: 3g; Protein: 37g; Carbohydrates: 64g; Cholesterol: 159mg; Sodium: 568mg; Fiber: 5g; Sugar: 6g

chicken pad thai

SERVES 6 / COOK TIME: 4 TO 6 HOURS ON LOW

GLUTEN-FREE • DAIRY-FREE

Thai is one of my favorite cuisines when eating out, and pad thai in particular is my go-to Thai dish. Between its spices and seasonings, flavorful meat, noodles, and fresh herbs, pad thai covers all the bases. Note that this dish does contain peanuts, which cannot be substituted, so if you have a peanut allergy, best sit this one out.

1 pound boneless, skinless chicken thighs, cut into strips

1 red or green bell pepper, seeded and chopped

1 onion, chopped

2 carrots, peeled and chopped

½ cup water

¼ cup low-sodium soy sauce, tamari, or coconut aminos

¼ cup peanut butter, melted in the microwave

3 tablespoons freshly squeezed lime juice

2 tablespoons rice vinegar

2 garlic cloves, minced

1 tablespoon ground cumin

½ tablespoon ground ginger

¼ tablespoon red pepper flakes

8 ounces brown rice noodles, cooked

1. Combine the chicken, bell pepper, onion, and carrots in the slow cooker.

2. In a medium bowl, whisk together the water, soy sauce, peanut butter, lime juice, rice vinegar, garlic, cumin, ginger, and red pepper flakes.

3. Pour the sauce into the slow cooker.

4. Cover and cook on low for 4 to 6 hours.

5. Remove the chicken and shred with two forks. Return the shredded chicken to the slow cooker and stir it in.

6. Serve on top of the rice noodles.

Tip: You can make this vegetarian by omitting the chicken and adding diced tofu. If you choose this option, stir in the tofu at the end, approximately 30 minutes before serving, so it's heated through.

PER SERVING Calories: 308; Total Fat: 9g; Saturated Fat: 2g; Protein: 19g; Carbohydrates: 37g; Cholesterol: 63mg; Sodium: 195mg; Fiber: 3g; Sugar: 3g

louisiana jambalaya

SERVES 6 / COOK TIME: 5 TO 7 HOURS ON LOW, PLUS 20 TO 30 MINUTES ON HIGH

GLUTEN-FREE • DAIRY-FREE

Originally from Louisiana, jambalaya is a dish that evolved from Spanish and French cuisines. In general, jambalaya consists of various meats and vegetables cooked with rice in broth in a Creole or Cajun style. This version is Creole, also called "red jambalaya." The name refers to the diced tomatoes used to create the sauce in which to cook the rice.

2 pounds boneless, skinless chicken thighs

¾ pound lean smoked sausage, thinly sliced

1 (28-ounce) can diced tomatoes, with their juice

2 cups low-sodium chicken broth

1 red or green bell pepper, seeded and diced

1 onion, diced

2 celery stalks, chopped

4 garlic cloves, minced

4 teaspoons Cajun seasoning

½ teaspoon dried thyme

½ teaspoon dried oregano

½ teaspoon freshly ground black pepper

½ teaspoon cayenne pepper

2 cups brown rice

1. Combine the chicken, sausage, tomatoes with their juice, broth, bell pepper, onion, celery, garlic, and seasonings in the slow cooker and mix well.

2. Cover and cook on low for 5 to 7 hours.

3. Remove the chicken and shred with two forks. Return the shredded chicken to the slow cooker and stir in the brown rice.

4. Cover and cook on high for 20 to 30 minutes, or until the rice is tender.

Tip: Jambalaya is similar to gumbo, except it doesn't include shrimp. You can add peeled and deveined shrimp if you want; just add them when you add the rice so they don't turn mushy.

PER SERVING Calories: 599; Total Fat: 24g; Saturated Fat: 7g; Protein: 43g; Carbohydrates: 59g; Cholesterol: 161mg; Sodium: 899mg; Fiber: 5g; Sugar: 9g

mexican green chile rice

SERVES 4 / COOK TIME: 6 TO 8 HOURS ON LOW

GLUTEN-FREE • VEGAN • DAIRY-FREE

Most people think of Spanish or Mexican rice as a side dish, but I like to eat it as a main course. Most vegetarians would agree that it can be quite filling—not to mention full of flavor—on its own. In addition to adding heat to this recipe, green chiles are loaded with antioxidants and vitamin C, which help maintain a healthy immune system. This Mexican dish is traditionally prepared by sautéing the rice in a skillet until golden brown, but I find that the slow cooker cooks the rice perfectly.

Cooking spray

1 cup brown rice

2 cups low-sodium vegetable broth

Juice of 1 lime

1 (15-ounce) can diced tomatoes, with their juice

1 (4-ounce) can diced green chiles, drained

1 teaspoon dried oregano

1 teaspoon ground cumin

1 teaspoon salt

½ teaspoon freshly ground black pepper

½ teaspoon garlic powder

½ teaspoon chili powder

Chopped fresh cilantro, for garnish

1. Coat the slow cooker generously with cooking spray.

2. Combine all the ingredients in the slow cooker and mix well.

3. Cover and cook on low for 6 to 8 hours. Garnish with cilantro before serving.

Tip: If you want to add meat, stir in 8 ounces cooked ground meat of your choice before serving.

PER SERVING Calories: 218; Total Fat: 2g; Saturated Fat: 0g; Protein: 6g; Carbohydrates: 45g; Cholesterol: 0mg; Sodium: 742mg; Fiber: 3g; Sugar: 4g

tex-mex quinoa bowl

SERVES 4 / COOK TIME: 8 HOURS ON LOW

GLUTEN-FREE • VEGAN • DAIRY-FREE

I'm a big fan of convenient one-pot bowls, especially when they're healthy. This recipe is exactly that: all your favorite Tex-Mex flavors combined with vegetables and quinoa. If you don't want to use quinoa, feel free to swap in brown rice.

1 cup quinoa, rinsed and drained

2 cups low-sodium vegetable broth

1 (15-ounce) can black beans, rinsed and drained

1 (15-ounce) can corn, drained

1 red or green bell pepper, seeded and chopped

1 small red onion, chopped

1 garlic clove, minced

¼ cup chopped fresh cilantro

1½ teaspoons ground cumin

1 teaspoon chili powder

1 teaspoon salt

½ teaspoon freshly ground black pepper

1. Combine all the ingredients in the slow cooker and mix well.
2. Cover and cook on low for 8 hours.

Tip: In addition to being gluten-free, quinoa provides a great vegetarian option for protein and is one of the few plant foods to contain all nine essential amino acids.

PER SERVING Calories: 305; Total Fat: 4g; Saturated Fat: 1g; Protein: 15g; Carbohydrates: 56g; Cholesterol: 0mg; Sodium: 728mg; Fiber: 11g; Sugar: 5g

mexican casserole with grains, beans, corn, and tomatoes

SERVES 4 / COOK TIME: 6 TO 8 HOURS ON LOW, PLUS 6 TO 8 HOURS ON LOW

GLUTEN-FREE • VEGAN • DAIRY-FREE

Although I'm suggesting quinoa for this dish, the choice is really up to you: quinoa, brown rice, jasmine rice all work well with approximately the same liquid amounts. Don't be concerned about the lack of broth or water to cook the grain. The liquid from the tomatoes and enchilada sauce will provide more than enough. If you don't have time to make the enchilada sauce, simply use a can of your favorite brand.

FOR THE ENCHILADA SAUCE

1 onion, chopped

3 garlic cloves, minced

2 cups low-sodium chicken or
  vegetable broth

1 (15-ounce) can diced tomatoes,
  with their juice

1 (8-ounce) can tomato sauce

1 tablespoon freshly squeezed
  lemon juice

1½ teaspoons chili powder

1 teaspoon dried oregano

1 teaspoon ground cumin

1 teaspoon salt

1 teaspoon freshly ground
  black pepper

FOR THE CASSEROLE

1 cup quinoa, rinsed and drained

1 (28-ounce) can diced tomatoes,
  with their juice

1 (15-ounce) can black beans,
  rinsed and drained

1 (15-ounce) can corn, drained

....

PER SERVING Calories: 396; Total Fat: 6g;
Saturated Fat: 1g; Protein: 20g;
Carbohydrates: 73g; Cholesterol: 0mg;
Sodium: 1,403mg; Fiber: 16g; Sugar: 16g

TO MAKE THE ENCHILADA SAUCE

1. Combine all the sauce ingredients in the slow cooker and mix well.
2. Cover and cook on low for 4 to 6 hours.
3. Transfer the sauce to a blender and blend to reach the desired consistency. (Remove the center cap from the blender lid, and hold a dish towel firmly over the hole while blending to allow the steam to escape.)

TO MAKE THE CASSEROLE

1. Combine the quinoa, tomatoes with their juice, black beans, corn, and enchilada sauce in the slow cooker and mix well.
2. Cover and cook on low for 6 to 8 hours.

Tip: To top this casserole, the sky is the limit: chopped scallions, fresh cilantro, shredded cheese, sliced olives—whatever your preference. I like to add my favorite taco toppings in line with the flavors of classic Mexican cuisine.

red beans and rice with andouille sausage

SERVES 8 / COOK TIME: 9 TO 11 HOURS ON LOW

GLUTEN-FREE • DAIRY-FREE

"Red beans and rice didn't miss her." Did anyone else just sing that in their head? Red beans and rice may sound like just two ingredients, but it's so much more. Featuring vegetables as well as sausage, this recipe is not just a side dish or starter, but a full one-pot meal.

1 medium onion diced

1 red or green bell pepper seeded and diced

2 celery stalks, chopped

2 garlic cloves, minced

12 ounces andouille sausage, thinly sliced

1 pound dried red kidney beans, soaked overnight and drained

1 teaspoon salt

½ teaspoon freshly ground black pepper

1 teaspoon chopped fresh thyme or ½ teaspoon dried thyme

1 bay leaf

8 cups water

8 cups cooked brown rice, for serving

1. Combine all the ingredients in the slow cooker and mix well.

2. Cover and cook on low for 9 to 11 hours.

3. Remove the bay leaf and stir.

4. Serve with the brown rice.

> **Tip:** Hold the sodium! Ditch the canned beans and use dried. You'll not only reduce your sodium intake, but dried beans are usually cheaper as well. Just soak them overnight before using. If you do use canned, be sure to rinse and drain them first.

PER SERVING Calories: 565; Total Fat: 14g; Saturated Fat: 5g; Protein: 26g; Carbohydrates: 84g; Cholesterol: 24mg; Sodium: 830mg; Fiber: 13g; Sugar: 3g

vegetable lo mein

SERVES 6 / COOK TIME: 6 TO 8 HOURS ON LOW

GLUTEN-FREE • VEGETARIAN • DAIRY-FREE

This recipe features the vegetables I like to use in lo mein, but feel free to heap this dish up with your own favorite vegetables. While this is a vegetarian dish, you can certainly add meat if you like. Add approximately 1 pound of your favorite raw protein in with the vegetables. Once the meal is done cooking, the meat should be so tender it shreds with a fork.

4 cups broccoli florets

3 carrots, peeled and julienned

3 celery stalks, chopped

1 cup snow peas

1 (8-ounce) can sliced
water chestnuts, drained

1 (15-ounce) can baby corn, drained

½ cup low-sodium soy sauce, tamari,
or coconut aminos

2 tablespoons honey

1 tablespoon oyster sauce

2 teaspoons chili paste

1 teaspoon toasted sesame oil

2 garlic cloves, minced

½ teaspoon ground ginger

1 pound spaghetti or linguine,
gluten-free if desired, cooked

....

PER SERVING Calories: 455; Total Fat: 4g;
Saturated Fat: 0g; Protein: 17g;
Carbohydrates: 95g; Cholesterol: 1mg;
Sodium: 949mg; Fiber: 11g; Sugar: 13g

1. Combine the broccoli, carrots, celery, snow peas, water chestnuts, and baby corn in the slow cooker.

2. In a medium bowl, whisk together the soy sauce, honey, oyster sauce, chili paste, sesame oil, garlic, and ginger.

3. Pour the sauce into the slow cooker and mix well.

4. Cover and cook on low for 6 to 8 hours.

5. Stir in the cooked pasta before serving.

Tip: For a heartier but still vegetarian dish, toss in some diced tofu or tempeh with the vegetables.

spinach and mushroom lasagna

SERVES 6 / COOK TIME: 6 TO 8 HOURS ON LOW

GLUTEN-FREE • VEGETARIAN

Lasagna was one of the first recipes I made when I got my first slow cooker. I had watched people make this dish using the traditional oven method, and it always involved so many steps. I couldn't believe that a slow cooker could make all that prep unnecessary, but it's true.

Cooking spray

1 (15-ounce) container low-fat ricotta cheese

2 cups shredded mozzarella cheese

1 cup chopped mushrooms

1 cup chopped spinach

2 garlic cloves, minced

1 tablespoon Italian Seasoning (page 100)

3 cups Marinara Sauce (page 73), or store-bought

9 lasagna noodles, gluten-free if desired

1 tablespoon grated Parmesan cheese, for serving

....

PER SERVING Calories: 488; Total Fat: 9g; Saturated Fat: 6g; Protein: 24g; Carbohydrates: 87g; Cholesterol: 30mg; Sodium: 442mg; Fiber: 3g; Sugar: 11g

1. Coat the slow cooker generously with cooking spray.

2. In a medium bowl, mix the ricotta, mozzarella, mushrooms, spinach, garlic, and Italian seasoning.

3. Spread ½ cup of the marinara sauce in the bottom of the slow cooker.

4. Add a layer of noodles, breaking them up to make them fit.

5. Add a layer of the cheese mixture.

6. Repeat the layers until all the ingredients are used.

7. Cover and cook on low for 6 to 8 hours.

8. Turn off the slow cooker and let the lasagna rest for 30 minutes.

9. Sprinkle with the Parmesan cheese before serving.

Tip: You can use kale instead of spinach, and other vegetables in addition to or in place of the mushrooms. If you like, you can double up on the vegetables or even the cheese.

meat and cheese stuffed shells

SERVES 4 / COOK TIME: 6 TO 8 HOURS ON LOW

GLUTEN-FREE

This is a fairly new recipe for me. If you can make lasagna and spaghetti in the slow cooker, why not stuffed shells, too? As long as there's enough liquid to the cover the pasta, you can cook any pasta efficiently with this method. If you find that the two jars of marinara sauce aren't enough to cover all your shells, simply add more.

¾ pound extra lean ground turkey

1 tablespoon Italian Seasoning
   (page 100)

1 onion, chopped

1 garlic clove, minced

1 large egg, lightly beaten

1½ cups shredded mozzarella cheese
   or ricotta cheese

6 ounces jumbo pasta shells,
   gluten-free if desired

3¾ cup Marinara Sauce (page 73),
   or store-bought, divided

¼ cup grated Parmesan cheese,
   plus extra for serving

....

PER SERVING Calories: 561; Total Fat: 13g; Saturated Fat: 7g; Protein: 46g; Carbohydrates: 70g; Cholesterol: 135mg; Sodium: 647mg; Fiber: 8g; Sugar: 12g

1. In a medium bowl, combine the ground turkey, Italian seasoning, onion, garlic, egg, and mozzarella, and mix well.

2. Stuff each shell evenly with the meat and cheese mixture.

3. Pour the first jar of sauce into the slow cooker. Place the stuffed shells on top of the sauce.

4. Pour the second jar of sauce over the shells, making sure they're completely covered. Sprinkle the Parmesan cheese on top.

5. Cover and cook on low for 6 to 8 hours.

Tip: This is another recipe you can jazz up as much as you like. Use your preferred ground meat—whether chicken, turkey, beef, or pork—and add more of your favorite vegetables.

turkey and kale stuffed manicotti

SERVES 6 / COOK TIME: 5 TO 7 HOURS ON LOW

GLUTEN-FREE

This recipe is very similar to Meat and Cheese Stuffed Shells (page 67): same concept, just different ingredients. Don't eat dairy? Omit the cheese and add more vegetables.

1 pound lean ground turkey

1 cup chopped kale

1 cup low-fat cottage cheese

2 cups shredded mozzarella cheese, divided

2 tablespoons Italian Seasoning (page 100)

8 ounces manicotti, gluten-free if desired

6 cups Marinara Sauce (page 73), or store-bought

....

PER SERVING Calories: 314; Total Fat: 6g; Saturated Fat: 2g; Protein: 37g; Carbohydrates: 49g; Cholesterol: 55mg; Sodium: 576mg; Fiber: 2g; Sugar: 6g

1. In a medium bowl, combine the ground turkey, kale, cottage cheese, 1 cup of mozzarella cheese, and Italian seasoning.

2. Transfer the mixture to a large plastic bag and seal. Cut a corner off the bottom of the bag.

3. Squeeze the mixture into each manicotti until full.

4. Spread 1 or 2 tablespoons of marinara sauce in the bottom of the slow cooker. Place the stuffed manicotti shells on top. Pour the remaining sauce on top of the shells, ensuring that all the shells are covered.

5. Cover and cook on low for 5 to 7 hours.

6. During the last 30 minutes of cook time, top the stuffed shells with the remaining 1 cup of mozzarella cheese, re-cover, and finish cooking.

Tip: This recipe can be modified with slightly different ingredients depending on your taste. For example, you can use ground chicken instead of turkey and spinach rather than kale.

butternut squash risotto

SERVES 6 / COOK TIME: 6 TO 8 HOURS ON LOW

GLUTEN-FREE • VEGETARIAN

Most people associate butternut squash with fall, but this risotto recipe is so light and healthy, it's perfect to serve year-round. I like to buy my butternut squash already peeled and chopped. You'll find this in the produce section of most grocery stores. And yes, you can use frozen butternut squash interchangeably in this recipe.

2 pounds butternut squash, peeled and diced

1½ cups brown rice

4 cups low-sodium vegetable broth

2 teaspoons extra-virgin olive oil

1 teaspoon ghee (optional)

1 onion, chopped

2 garlic cloves, chopped

1 teaspoon dried sage

1 teaspoon salt

½ teaspoon ground cumin

½ teaspoon freshly ground black pepper

¼ cup grated Parmesan cheese

....

PER SERVING Calories: 295; Total Fat: 5g; Saturated Fat: 2g; Protein: 8g; Carbohydrates: 57g; Cholesterol: 5mg; Sodium: 487mg; Fiber: 5g; Sugar: 4g

1. Combine all the ingredients in the slow cooker and mix well.

2. Cover and cook on low for 6 to 8 hours.

3. Add the cheese and stir to combine.

Tip: This isn't the risotto you think you know. Since the rice is cooked low and slow, it will be a lot softer than the stove top variety.

mushroom risotto

SERVES 6 / COOK TIME: 6 TO 8 HOURS ON LOW

GLUTEN-FREE • VEGAN • DAIRY-FREE

Every time I make this recipe, I get compliments. People think this dish requires hours of slaving over the stove. It didn't. It's just the slow cooker working its magic. I like to use Parmesan cheese—preferably Parmigiano-Reggiano—for risotto, but mozzarella or even Gruyère make good substitutes, if you prefer—or leave out the cheese entirely for a dairy-free, vegan risotto.

1¾ cups brown rice

4 cups low-sodium vegetable broth

2 tablespoons extra-virgin olive oil

8 ounces mushrooms, sliced

1 small onion, chopped

2 garlic cloves, minced

1 teaspoon salt

¼ teaspoon freshly ground
   black pepper

Grated Asiago or Parmesan cheese
   (optional)

....

PER SERVING Calories: 265; Total Fat: 6g; Saturated Fat: 1g; Protein: 7g; Carbohydrates: 46g; Cholesterol: 0mg; Sodium: 439mg; Fiber: 3g; Sugar: 1g

1. Combine all the ingredients in the slow cooker and mix well.

2. Cover and cook on low for 6 to 8 hours.

3. Add the cheese (if using), stir, and re-cover until melted.

Tip: Most people don't realize that mushrooms are an excellent source of protein, vitamin C, and iron. To obtain the mushrooms' nutritional benefits, however, you need to cook them.

classic spaghetti marinara and meatballs

SERVES 6 / COOK TIME: 6 TO 8 HOURS ON LOW

GLUTEN-FREE • DAIRY-FREE

Here is another classic pasta dish adapted to the slow cooker. Most people don't think of spaghetti as being healthy, but it definitely has its healthy elements, especially when you use whole-wheat pasta—a good source of vitamins, minerals, and of course fiber. Adding meatballs is optional but recommended. While you can certainly make homemade meatballs, this recipe calls for frozen meatballs. You can find natural frozen meatballs in your grocery store or health food store.

Cooking spray

6 cups Marinara Sauce (page 73),
    or store-bought

1½ teaspoons extra-virgin olive oil

2 garlic cloves, minced

2 teaspoons Italian Seasoning
    (page 100)

½ teaspoon salt

1 pound spaghetti, gluten-free
    if desired

1 (16-ounce) bag frozen meatballs
    (optional)

....

PER SERVING Calories: 342; Total Fat: 7g;
Saturated Fat: 2g; Protein: 15g;
Carbohydrates: 74g; Cholesterol: 5mg;
Sodium: 710mg; Fiber: 2g; Sugar: 7g

1. Coat the slow cooker generously with cooking spray.

2. Combine the marinara sauce, olive oil, garlic, Italian seasoning, and salt in the slow cooker and mix well.

3. Add the spaghetti, breaking it up into smaller pieces if needed, and the meatballs, if using. Mix well to ensure that all the spaghetti is well coated with sauce.

4. Cover and cook on low for 6 to 8 hours.

Tip: Adding the oil helps prevent the spaghetti from sticking. You may also want to separate the strands if you see them beginning to stick.

meat and veggie deep-dish pizza

SERVES 4 / COOK TIME: 6 TO 8 HOURS ON LOW

A lot of slow cooker pizza recipes are essentially just pasta with cheese. This is an actual pizza with real crust cooked in the slow cooker. Each time I make this recipe, I like to switch up the flavors of my pizza in different ways. For example, you can use pepperoni or sausage instead of ground beef. Sub in onions, mushrooms, or olives for the bell pepper. Same with the crust—use regular pizza dough, whole wheat, or gluten free. Each will produce an equally fantastic result.

Cooking spray

1 (13.8-ounce) can refrigerated pizza dough

1¼ cup Marinara Sauce (page 73), or store-bought

8 ounces extra-lean ground beef

1 red or green bell pepper, seeded and diced

4 cups shredded low-fat mozzarella cheese

....

PER SERVING Calories: 444; Total Fat: 10g; Saturated Fat: 5g; Protein: 30g; Carbohydrates: 48g; Cholesterol: 50mg; Sodium: 527mg; Fiber: 4g; Sugar: 6g

1. Coat the slow cooker generously with cooking spray and line the bottom with parchment paper.

2. Press the dough into the bottom of the slow cooker and 1 or 2 inches up the sides.

3. Top with the sauce, ground beef, bell pepper, and cheese.

4. Cover and cook on low for 6 to 8 hours.

> **Tip:** This recipe somewhat resembles a deep-dish pizza—think Chicago rather than New York style. In addition to spraying the slow cooker with cooking spray, I suggest you also line it with parchment paper—this will make it easier to remove the pizza when it's done cooking.

A WORD ON STORE-BOUGHT MARINARA SAUCE

I use marinara sauce a lot in my slow cooker recipes, but jarred tomato sauces are often loaded with added sugars. This slow cooker version is easy to make ahead in bulk and freeze for the right time. If you don't have time to make a batch of sauce in advance, check the labels of store-bought sauces and look for sugar-free options.

marinara sauce

YIELD: 8 CUPS / COOK TIME: 6 TO 8 HOURS ON LOW

GLUTEN-FREE • DAIRY-FREE

2 (28-ounce) cans crushed tomatoes

1 cup Beef or Chicken Bone Broth (page 13), or store-bought

1 large onion, diced

4 garlic cloves, crushed

5 tablespoons tomato paste

1 bay leaf

2 teaspoons oregano

1½ teaspoons salt

1 teaspoon dried thyme

1 teaspoon dried basil

½ teaspoon freshly ground black pepper

½ teaspoon red pepper flakes

1. Add all the ingredients to the slow cooker. Stir to mix well.

2. Cook on low for 6 to 8 hours.

3. Remove the bay leaf before serving.

4. Optional: pour the sauce in a blender and blend until it reaches your desired consistency. An immersion blender directly in the slow cooker also works well for this.

PER SERVING (1 CUP) Calories: 57; Total Fat: 0g; Saturated Fat: 0g; Protein: 2g; Carbohydrates: 12g; Cholesterol: 0mg; Sodium: 512mg; Fiber: 2g; Sugar: 5g

Vegetarian Bean Cholent *page 90*

beans, lentils, and vegetables

summer vegetables

SERVES 4 / COOK TIME: 6 TO 8 HOURS ON LOW

GLUTEN-FREE • VEGAN • DAIRY-FREE

Summer is my favorite season but don't get me wrong: This is a year-round dish. When I make this in winter I simply call it "Winter Vegetables." I encourage you to use whatever vegetables are in season during the particular time of year when you're making this recipe—it's the key to maximum flavor.

1 (15-ounce) can diced tomatoes,
   with their juice

1 pound zucchini, chopped

1 pound eggplant, chopped

1 pound green beans, trimmed

1 pound red potatoes, chopped

¼ cup freshly squeezed lemon juice

¼ cup low-sodium soy sauce, tamari,
   or coconut aminos

2 tablespoons extra-virgin olive oil

2 tablespoons Worcestershire sauce

1 garlic clove, minced

½ teaspoon salt

½ teaspoon freshly ground
   black pepper

1. Pour the diced tomatoes with their juice into the slow cooker.

2. Add the vegetables and potatoes on top of the tomatoes.

3. In a medium bowl, whisk together the lemon juice, soy sauce, olive oil, Worcestershire, garlic, salt, and pepper.

4. Pour the sauce into the slow cooker, making sure all the vegetables are covered.

5. Cover and cook on low for 6 to 8 hours, or until the vegetables are soft.

6. Stir before serving.

Tip: Try to cut all the vegetables into similar-size pieces so they cook evenly.

PER SERVING Calories: 266; Total Fat: 8g; Saturated Fat: 1g; Protein: 10g; Carbohydrates: 44g; Cholesterol: 0mg; Sodium: 1,035mg; Fiber: 13g; Sugar: 13g

ratatouille

SERVES 4 / COOK TIME: 6 TO 8 HOURS ON LOW

GLUTEN-FREE • VEGAN • DAIRY-FREE

The first time I tasted ratatouille, I knew it would make a fantastic slow cooker recipe: vegetables cooked slowly in a tomato-based sauce with fresh herbs. Doesn't get any easier than that! Like many slow cooker dishes, ratatouille has tons of variations because of the wide variety of vegetables one might include. This recipe is a simple version using basic, common ingredients.

1 (15-ounce) can diced tomatoes, with their juice

¼ cup low-sodium vegetable broth

2 garlic cloves, minced

1 tablespoon extra-virgin olive oil

1 teaspoon salt

½ teaspoon dried tarragon

½ teaspoon dried rosemary

½ teaspoon dried thyme

½ teaspoon dried basil

1 bay leaf

2 pounds eggplant, peeled and chopped

1 large onion, chopped

2 medium zucchini, chopped

1 red or green bell pepper, seeded and chopped

1. In a medium bowl, combine the tomatoes with their juice, broth, garlic, olive oil, and seasonings, and mix well. Pour the sauce into the slow cooker.

2. Add the eggplant, onion, zucchini, and bell pepper on top of the sauce.

3. Cover and cook on low for 6 to 8 hours.

4. Remove the bay leaf before serving.

Tip: Dice, chop, slice, cut into rounds—whatever shape you like for your ratatouille vegetables is up to you.

PER SERVING Calories: 150; Total Fat: 5g; Saturated Fat: 1g; Protein: 5g; Carbohydrates: 27g; Cholesterol: 0mg; Sodium: 608mg; Fiber: 12g; Sugar: 14g

ethiopian cabbage

SERVES 6 / COOK TIME: 6 TO 8 HOURS ON LOW

GLUTEN-FREE • VEGAN • PALEO • DAIRY-FREE

This recipe hands down changed my perspective on cabbage. Growing up, I always thought that cabbage could only be boiled and must therefore be bland, which is a shame, because cabbage is not only a fairly inexpensive vegetable but also a great source of vitamin C and manganese. I love eating at Ethiopian restaurants, and when I tried their cabbage, a lightbulb went off. Cabbage can be flavorful! This recipe is proof.

½ cup water

1 head green cabbage, cored and chopped

1 pound sweet potatoes, peeled and chopped

3 carrots, peeled and chopped

1 onion, sliced

1 teaspoon extra-virgin olive oil

½ teaspoon ground turmeric

½ teaspoon ground cumin

¼ teaspoon ground ginger

....

PER SERVING Calories: 155; Total Fat: 1g; Saturated Fat: 0g; Protein: 4g; Carbohydrates: 35g; Cholesterol: 0g; Sodium: 56g; Fiber: 8g; Sugar: 8g

1. Pour the water into the slow cooker.

2. In a medium bowl, combine the cabbage, sweet potatoes, carrots, and onion. Add the olive oil, turmeric, cumin, and ginger, and toss until the vegetables are well coated.

3. Transfer the vegetable mixture to the slow cooker.

4. Cover and cook on low for 6 to 8 hours.

Tip: The slow cooker will be filled to the rim, but don't worry, the cabbage will cook down considerably. This is a unique side dish to serve at your next holiday dinner.

spaghetti squash casserole

SERVES 4 / COOK TIME: 6 TO 8 HOURS ON LOW

GLUTEN-FREE • VEGETARIAN

I wish I'd known about spaghetti squash when I was child—I would have gladly eaten it with no insisting from my mother necessary! Spaghetti squash is the perfect low-carb alternative to pasta: Once it's cooked, you scrape out the strands of the squash to resemble spaghetti noodles. This dish can be customized to include as few or as many ingredients as you like.

1 medium spaghetti squash, cooked (see Tip)

8 ounces kale or spinach leaves

3 cups Marinara Sauce (page 73), or store-bought

3 garlic cloves, minced

2 tablespoons Italian Seasoning (page 100), divided

1 teaspoon dried basil (optional)

2 cups shredded mozzarella cheese

5 ounces pepperoni (optional)

....

PER SERVING Calories: 243; Total Fat: 6g; Saturated Fat: 3g; Protein: 12g; Carbohydrates: 48g; Cholesterol: 11mg; Sodium: 473mg; Fiber: 7g; Sugar: 18g

1. When the spaghetti squash is cool enough to handle, cut it in half and shred the flesh with a fork. Transfer the spaghetti squash strands to the slow cooker.

2. Add the kale, marinara sauce, garlic, 1 tablespoon of Italian seasoning, and basil (if using), and mix well.

3. Top with the cheese, pepperoni (if using), and remaining 1 tablespoon of Italian seasoning.

4. Cover and cook on low for 6 to 8 hours.

Tip: The easiest way to cook a spaghetti squash is in the microwave. Pierce the squash several times with a fork. Microwave for 5 minutes, flip, and microwave for 3 to 5 minutes, depending on the size of the spaghetti squash. Wear oven mitts when removing the squash from the microwave, as it will be very hot.

cinnamon-honey acorn squash

SERVES 4 / COOK TIME: 6 TO 8 HOURS ON LOW

GLUTEN-FREE • VEGETARIAN • PALEO

Cinnamon and honey are a fantastic combination, especially on squash and potatoes. But I appreciate that the cinnamon-honey combo might be a little too sweet for some people. If that's a concern, just cut the honey measurement in half. This recipe lists ghee (clarified butter) as an ingredient. If you're following a dairy-free diet and therefore avoiding butter, substitute whatever oil fits your dietary needs. One acorn squash should fit in an oval 6-quart slow cooker.

1 acorn squash

2 tablespoons extra-virgin olive oil

½ cup water

1½ teaspoons cinnamon

½ teaspoon salt

1 teaspoon freshly ground
   black pepper

2 tablespoons honey or maple syrup

2 tablespoons extra-virgin olive oil

1 teaspoon ghee

....

PER SERVING Calories: 214; Total Fat: 15g; Saturated Fat: 3g; Protein: 1g; Carbohydrates: 23g; Cholesterol: 3mg; Sodium: 295mg; Fiber: 4g; Sugar: 9g

1. Cut the acorn squash in half lengthwise. Scoop out the seeds and stringy fiber. Drizzle the oil over the cut surfaces of the squash.

2. Pour the water into the slow cooker.

3. Place the acorn squash halves, cut-side up, in the slow cooker.

4. Sprinkle the cinnamon, salt, and pepper over the squash halves, then drizzle them with the honey.

5. Add ½ teaspoon ghee on top of each.

6. Cover and cook on low for 6 to 8 hours.

Tip: This is a healthy alternative to the sweet potato and marshmallow casserole usually served as a holiday side dish, particularly on Thanksgiving.

black-eyed peas and spinach

SERVES 4 / COOK TIME: 8 HOURS ON LOW

GLUTEN-FREE • DAIRY-FREE

My mom taught me to eat black-eyed peas every New Year's Day for good luck. I'm generally not that lucky, but it's still a tradition that stuck with me. When I started cooking for myself, I quickly realized that the last thing I wanted to do was cook on New Year's Day after partying all night on New Year's Eve. Then it dawned on me: Just use my slow cooker! Now I put all the ingredients of this dish in my slow cooker every New Year's Eve and—like magic—wake up January 1 to my lucky meal.

1 cup black-eyed peas, soaked overnight and drained

2 cups low-sodium chicken broth

1 (15-ounce) can diced tomatoes, with their juice

8 ounces ham, chopped

1 onion, chopped

2 garlic cloves, minced

1 teaspoon dried oregano

1 teaspoon salt

½ teaspoon freshly ground black pepper

½ teaspoon ground mustard

1 bay leaf

1. Combine all the ingredients in the slow cooker and mix well.

2. Cover and cook on low for 8 hours.

3. Remove the bay leaf before serving.

Tip: You can use your slow cooker for soaking the peas overnight before you use them. Just be sure to drain the water completely before you start the recipe.

PER SERVING Calories: 209; Total Fat: 6g; Saturated Fat: 2g; Protein: 17g; Carbohydrates: 22g; Cholesterol: 32mg; Sodium: 1,366mg; Fiber: 3g; Sugar: 4g

cowboy beans

SERVES 4 / COOK TIME: 8 HOURS ON LOW

GLUTEN-FREE • VEGETARIAN • DAIRY-FREE

It is true what they say, beans are good for your heart. The more you eat, the more fiber you take in! A high-fiber diet may help reduce the risk of obesity, heart disease, and diabetes. This is a great vegan recipe, but non-vegetarians who can't resist can go ahead and throw in some meat. If you want to use dried beans, be sure to soak them overnight.

1 (15-ounce) can pinto beans, rinsed and drained

1 (15-ounce) can kidney beans, rinsed and drained

1 (15-ounce) can great northern beans, rinsed and drained

2 red or green bell peppers, seeded and diced

2 large tomatoes, diced

1 large onion, diced

3 garlic cloves, minced

¼ cup yellow or Dijon mustard

¼ cup honey or maple syrup

2 teaspoons salt

1 teaspoon freshly ground black pepper

1 teaspoon ground cumin

½ teaspoon chili powder

1. Combine all the ingredients in the slow cooker and mix well.

2. Cover and cook on low for 8 hours.

Tip: For an extra punch of flavor, I like to add a pound or two of crumbled cooked bacon to my beans. You can also add browned ground beef, chicken, or pork. Or add *both* bacon and ground meat! The choice is yours.

PER SERVING Calories: 287; Total Fat: 2g; Saturated Fat: 0g; Protein: 10g; Carbohydrates: 49g; Cholesterol: 0mg; Sodium: 1,441mg; Fiber: 11g; Sugar: 26g

aloo palak

SERVES 4 / COOK TIME: 6 TO 8 HOURS ON LOW

GLUTEN-FREE • VEGAN • PALEO • DAIRY-FREE

Aloo palak is a traditional Indian dish composed of potatoes and spinach. As you've undoubtedly noticed by now, this cookbook includes a lot of Indian recipes, because slow cookers are excellent for preparing Indian dishes. Most recipes just call for putting everything in, stirring, and cooking. This might not result in the most visually appealing dish, but it will taste great.

2 pounds red potatoes, chopped, or sweet potatoes, peeled and chopped

1 small onion, diced

1 red or green bell pepper, seeded and diced

¼ cup chopped fresh cilantro

⅓ cup low-sodium vegetable broth

1 teaspoon salt

½ teaspoon garam masala

½ teaspoon ground cumin

¼ teaspoon ground turmeric

¼ teaspoon ground coriander

¼ teaspoon freshly ground black pepper

2 pounds fresh spinach, chopped

1. Combine the potatoes, onion, bell pepper, cilantro, broth, and seasonings in the slow cooker and mix well.

2. Add the spinach on top.

3. Cover and cook on low for 6 to 8 hours, or until the potatoes are soft.

Tip: You might have to push the spinach down to make it all fit. Not to worry—it will shrink tremendously. Serve this dish over the rice of your choice.

PER SERVING Calories: 205; Total Fat: 1g; Saturated Fat: 0g; Protein: 9g; Carbohydrates: 44g; Cholesterol: 0g; Sodium: 779mg; Fiber: 11g; Sugar: 4g

coconut jackfruit and chickpeas

SERVES 4 / COOK TIME: 6 TO 8 HOURS ON LOW

GLUTEN-FREE • VEGAN • DAIRY-FREE

The first time I tasted jackfruit, I almost thought I was eating meat. Not only does it look like meat, but it has a meaty texture. However, it is definitely a fruit—it's also low-calorie, low-fat, and a great source of dietary fiber, iron, calcium, and potassium. It's extremely versatile to cook with, and it makes a great slow cooker meal. The toughness of the plant is perfect for the low-and-slow method.

1 (20-ounce) can young jackfruit in water, drained

1 (15-ounce) can chickpeas, rinsed and drained

1 (15-ounce) can diced tomatoes, with their juice

1 (15-ounce) can full-fat coconut milk or coconut cream

1 cup low-sodium vegetable broth

1 onion, diced

3 garlic cloves, minced

Handful fresh cilantro leaves

2 teaspoons curry powder

1½ teaspoons ground ginger

1 teaspoon ground coriander

½ teaspoon ground turmeric

½ teaspoon salt

1. Combine all the ingredients in the slow cooker and mix well.

2. Cover and cook on low for 6 to 8 hours.

Tip: This recipe works particularly well served over rice. If you like spicy food, a teaspoon of chili powder takes it up a notch in heat.

PER SERVING Calories: 536; Total Fat: 37g; Saturated Fat: 26g; Protein: 18g; Carbohydrates: 38g; Cholesterol: 0mg; Sodium: 1,494mg; Fiber: 5g; Sugar: 11g

creamy cauliflower and sweet potatoes

SERVES 6 / COOK TIME: 6 TO 8 HOURS ON LOW

GLUTEN-FREE • VEGAN • PALEO • DAIRY-FREE

This recipe is based on aloo gobi, an Indian curry made from potatoes and cauliflower. It's one of those dishes that everyone has a different version of. Mine keeps the traditional flavors but makes a few ingredient swaps. For one, I replaced potatoes with sweet potatoes, making this Paleo-friendly. I like white sweet potatoes, but if you can't find them, you can use orange sweet potatoes instead, or even regular potatoes.

1 head cauliflower, trimmed and chopped

2 pounds sweet potatoes, peeled and chopped

1 onion, diced

3 garlic cloves, minced

½ cup chopped fresh cilantro

1 (15-ounce) can diced tomatoes, with their juice

1 (15-ounce) can coconut cream or full-fat coconut milk

2 teaspoons ground cumin

1 teaspoon ground ginger

1 teaspoon curry powder or garam masala

1 teaspoon salt

1 teaspoon ground turmeric

½ teaspoon freshly ground black pepper

1. Combine all the ingredients in the slow cooker and mix well.

2. Cover and cook on low for 6 to 8 hours.

Tip: You need to use fresh cauliflower for this recipe. Frozen vegetables work in many slow cooker recipes, but cauliflower can often be an exception—it just releases too much liquid.

PER SERVING Calories: 502; Total Fat: 28g; Saturated Fat: 22g; Protein: 8g; Carbohydrates: 58g; Cholesterol: 0mg; Sodium: 474mg; Fiber: 10g; Sugar: 8g

vegan coconut chickpeas

SERVES 4 / COOK TIME: 6 TO 8 HOURS ON LOW

GLUTEN-FREE • VEGAN • DAIRY-FREE

If I had to pick which cuisines contribute most to this dish, I would say Thai and Indian. These two cuisines make some the best curries around, and this recipe incorporates both. This dish is vegan but not lacking in flavor. Coconut cream or full-fat coconut replaces the dairy but provides a wonderful creaminess.

2 (15-ounce) cans chickpeas, rinsed and drained

1 (15-ounce) can full-fat coconut milk or coconut cream

Juice of 1 lime

8 ounces Roma tomatoes, diced

1 small onion, diced

2 garlic cloves, minced

1 tablespoon Thai red curry paste

1 teaspoon curry powder

1 teaspoon ground cumin

½ teaspoon salt

¼ teaspoon freshly ground black pepper

1. Combine all the ingredients in the slow cooker and mix well.

2. Cover and cook on low for 6 to 8 hours.

Tip: I've occasionally been told that this recipe can use more salt, so feel free to sprinkle additional salt on top according to your personal taste and diet.

PER SERVING Calories: 564; Total Fat: 43g; Saturated Fat: 34g; Protein: 11g; Carbohydrates: 35g; Cholesterol: 0mg; Sodium: 766mg; Fiber: 1g; Sugar: 12g

legume dal

SERVES 4 / COOK TIME: 6 TO 8 HOURS ON LOW

GLUTEN-FREE • VEGAN • DAIRY-FREE

This Indian recipe features a combination of three different types of lentils—black, red, and green. Packed with nutrients like fiber, protein, minerals, and vitamins, lentils are low in calories and contain almost no fat. They need soaking overnight before cooking, but the good news is that you can soak all three varieties together in your slow cooker. Just add enough water to cover them all, and place the entire pot in the fridge. The next morning when you're ready to start the recipe, drain off all the water, and your slow cooker will be ready for the other ingredients.

2 cups dried black, red, and green lentils, soaked overnight and drained

5 cups water

1 large tomato, diced

1 onion, diced

5 garlic cloves, minced

1 tablespoon ground cumin

1 teaspoon ground ginger

1 teaspoon ground turmeric

1 teaspoon curry powder

1 teaspoon salt

½ teaspoon freshly ground black pepper

1. Combine all the ingredients in the slow cooker and mix well.

2. Cover and cook on low for 6 to 8 hours.

Tip: These lentils taste great over rice or accompanied by naan or other bread that's compatible with your diet.

....

PER SERVING Calories: 375; Total Fat: 2g; Saturated Fat: 0g; Protein: 26g; Carbohydrates: 65g; Cholesterol: 0mg; Sodium: 603mg; Fiber: 31g; Sugar: 4g

lentils with butternut squash

SERVES 4 / COOK TIME: 6 TO 8 HOURS ON LOW

GLUTEN-FREE • VEGAN

Here lentils are paired with butternut squash—an excellent source of vitamins A and C, magnesium, and fiber. It also contains high amounts of manganese, which helps the body process fats, carbohydrates, and glucose. As they cook together, the butternut squash and lentils create an almost risotto-like consistency. Meanwhile, the flavors blend as they're slow-cooked over many hours. Remember to soak those high-fiber lentils! Use your preferred variety of lentils for this dish: red or green, or a combo of both.

1½ cups red and/or green lentils, soaked overnight and drained

8 ounces butternut squash, diced

4 cups water

1 (15-ounce) can diced tomatoes, with their juice

1 cup full-fat coconut milk

1 teaspoon ghee (optional)

1 onion, chopped

2 garlic cloves, minced

2 teaspoons ground cumin

1 teaspoon chili powder

1 teaspoon salt

½ teaspoon freshly ground black pepper

2 scallions, sliced, for garnish

1. Combine all the ingredients in the slow cooker and mix well.

2. Cover and cook low 6 to 8 hours.

3. Top with the scallions before serving.

Tip: I like to serve this over rice. Jasmine rice, brown rice, or whatever variety you prefer will work well.

PER SERVING Calories: 576; Total Fat: 24g; Saturated Fat: 19g; Protein: 23g; Carbohydrates: 66g; Cholesterol: 3mg; Sodium: 634mg; Fiber: 25g; Sugar: 10g

falafel

SERVES 4 / COOK TIME: 6 TO 8 HOURS ON LOW

GLUTEN-FREE • VEGETARIAN • DAIRY-FREE

Falafel is probably the last thing you'd expect to cook in the slow cooker, but trust me, it works. It even comes out nice and crispy. Since falafel's main ingredient is chickpeas, its health benefits are many—high in fiber and protein and relatively low in calories. I encourage you to use dried chickpeas to cut down on sodium and cost, but remember that you will need to soak them overnight.

Cooking spray

1 (15-ounce) can chickpeas, rinsed and drained

½ onion, chopped

2 garlic cloves, minced

3 tablespoons freshly squeezed lemon juice

1 large egg, lightly beaten

⅓ cup bread crumbs, gluten-free if desired

2 teaspoons dried parsley

2 teaspoons ground cumin

1 teaspoon ground coriander

1 teaspoon salt

¼ teaspoon freshly ground black pepper

1. Coat the bottom of your slow cooker generously with cooking spray.

2. Combine all the ingredients in a food processor and blend until smooth.

3. Form the falafel mixture into 1-inch balls and place them in a single layer in the slow cooker.

4. Cover and cook on low for 6 to 8 hours.

Tip: You might want to wet your hands when forming the falafel balls, because they will be rather sticky. This falafel tastes great served with fat-free Greek yogurt sauce.

PER SERVING Calories: 130; Total Fat: 3g; Saturated Fat: 1g; Protein: 6g; Carbohydrates: 20g; Cholesterol: 47mg; Sodium: 780mg; Fiber: 1g; Sugar: 6g

vegetarian bean cholent

SERVES 6 / COOK TIME: 12 TO 15 HOURS ON LOW

VEGETARIAN • DAIRY-FREE

Cholent is a hearty, traditional Jewish stew featuring beef, potatoes, and three different types of beans. It's perfect for the Sabbath, since it cooks overnight in the slow cooker. I usually make this with beef but sometimes without, as here, and it's still really tasty—and using potatoes and three kinds of beans makes this meal extremely hearty. Considering that beans are high in antioxidants, fiber, protein, B vitamins, iron, magnesium, potassium, copper, and zinc, they make it extra-nutritious, too! The beans need to be soaked overnight, but you can soak them all together.

1 pound red potatoes,
    cut into 1½-inch chunks

1 onion, peeled and cut
    into 1½-inch chunks

¾ cup pearl barley

⅓ cup dried kidney beans,
    soaked overnight and drained

⅓ cup dried great northern beans,
    soaked overnight and drained

⅓ cup dried pinto beans, soaked
    overnight and drained

3 cups low-sodium vegetable broth

2 tablespoons honey or maple syrup

2 tablespoons paprika

½ teaspoon salt

¼ teaspoon freshly ground
    black pepper

1. Combine the potatoes and onion in the bottom of the slow cooker.

2. Scatter the barley and beans on top.

3. Pour in the broth and honey, add the paprika, and sprinkle with the salt and pepper.

4. Add enough water to cover all the ingredients.

5. Cover and cook on low for 12 to 15 hours, stirring occasionally and adding more water if necessary.

Tip: For the potatoes, use a waxy variety like red potatoes or new potatoes. Since they are generally firmer, they will hold their shape better than russets during the long cooking process.

PER SERVING Calories: 290; Total Fat: 1g; Saturated Fat: 0g; Protein: 12g; Carbohydrates: 60g; Cholesterol: 0mg; Sodium: 241mg; Fiber: 12g; Sugar: 8g

baked beans with ham and green beans

SERVES 4 / COOK TIME: 8 HOURS ON LOW

You'll never want to buy canned beans again after you try this recipe. Homemade baked beans are not only super easy to prepare, but they also have half the sodium of canned. Adding in ham and green beans transforms this from side dish into complete meal.

2 ½ cups chicken broth

½ cup honey

¼ cup Ketchup (see page 122), or store-bought

1 tablespoon Dijon mustard

1 teaspoon salt

1 teaspoon freshly ground black pepper

2 cups dried great northern beans, pre-soaked, or 2 (15-ounce) cans, rinsed and drained

½ pound ham, chopped

½ pound green beans

1 small onion, chopped

1. Add the broth, honey, ketchup, mustard, salt, and pepper to the bottom of the slow cooker. Stir to mix well.

2. Add the great northern beans, ham, green beans, and onion.

3. Stir again until all the ingredients are well blended.

4. Cook on low for 6 to 8 hours.

Tip: These beans will thicken as they sit, especially while cooling, but there's no need to add any liquid. When you re-heat the beans, they will go back to their original consistency.

PER SERVING Calories: 327; Total fat: 6g; Saturated fat: 2g; Protein: 19g; Carbohydrates: 59g; Cholesterol: 34mg; Sodium: 2,056mg; Fiber: 10g; Sugars: 41g

Chicken Cacciatore *page 95*

chicken
and turkey

·····································

tomato-garlic chicken and herbs

SERVES 4 / COOK TIME: 5 TO 7 HOURS ON LOW

GLUTEN-FREE • PALEO • DAIRY-FREE

This is a terrific recipe to prepare in bulk and freeze. I like to use chicken thighs in this one, but you can use pretty much any cut of chicken, with or without skin and bones. To make this a complete one-pot meal, add 1 pound of diced red potatoes and a vegetable like green beans or broccoli.

3 pounds boneless, skinless chicken thighs

½ cup low-sodium chicken broth

2 cups cherry tomatoes, halved

4 garlic cloves, minced

2 teaspoons garlic salt

¼ teaspoon ground white pepper

2 tablespoons chopped fresh basil

2 tablespoons chopped fresh oregano

1. Combine all the ingredients in the slow cooker and mix well.

2. Cover and cook on low for 5 to 7 hours.

> **Tip:** Switch up the herbs! Rosemary and sage work well with this dish, too. If you use dried herbs instead of fresh, you'll want to use only about a third as much.

PER SERVING Calories: 425; Total Fat: 14g; Saturated Fat: 3g; Protein: 68g; Carbohydrates: 7g; Cholesterol: 285mg; Sodium: 314mg; Fiber: 2g; Sugar: 3g

chicken cacciatore

SERVES 4 / COOK TIME: 5 TO 7 HOURS ON LOW

GLUTEN-FREE • PALEO • DAIRY-FREE

This is a healthy version of an Italian classic. The perfect meal to serve your family or impress a date, this can also be a great recipe if you're on a weight-loss journey—it's amazingly low-fat, low-carb, and low-calorie. Traditionally, cacciatore is prepared using white wine. However, alcohol doesn't work well in the slow cooker, so I've replaced it here with low-sodium broth. If you prefer, you can also use water. This makes a satisfying meal served over brown rice.

1 (15-ounce) can crushed tomatoes

8 ounces mushrooms, sliced

2 red or green bell peppers, seeded and sliced

2 carrots, peeled and chopped

1 onion, sliced

3 garlic cloves, minced

½ cup low-sodium chicken broth or water

2 teaspoons dried oregano

2 teaspoons dried basil

1 teaspoon salt

1 teaspoon freshly ground black pepper

3 pounds boneless, skinless chicken thighs

1. Combine the crushed tomatoes, mushrooms, bell peppers, carrots, onion, garlic, broth, and seasonings in the slow cooker and mix well.

2. Add the chicken and mix again.

3. Cover and cook on low for 5 to 7 hours.

Tip: The slow cooker will contain a lot of juices when this has finished cooking. Before serving, pour some of these juices over the chicken.

PER SERVING Calories: 496; Total Fat: 14g; Saturated Fat: 3g; Protein: 72g; Carbohydrates: 22g; Cholesterol: 285mg; Sodium: 1,122mg; Fiber: 7g; Sugar: 13g

garlic-citrus chicken and potatoes

SERVES 4 / COOK TIME: 5 TO 7 HOURS ON LOW

GLUTEN-FREE • DAIRY-FREE

I love garlic and lemons and was inspired by a Cuban garlic-citrus marinade known as mojo to create this dish. I always seed the jalapeño, but it's up to you if you want to leave some or all in—just be aware that too many seeds will change the flavor of the dish. The garlic and citrus should be the star ingredients, not the jalapeño. In other words, this dish isn't meant to be too spicy.

1 onion, sliced

1 pound red potatoes, diced

2 pounds boneless, skinless chicken thighs

⅓ cup freshly squeezed lime juice

¼ cup freshly squeezed orange juice

2 tablespoons extra-virgin olive oil

7 garlic cloves, minced

1 teaspoon salt

1 teaspoon dried oregano

¼ teaspoon ground cumin

1 lemon, sliced

1 jalapeño, seeded and sliced

....

PER SERVING Calories: 431; Total Fat: 16g; Saturated Fat: 3g; Protein: 47g; Carbohydrates: 25g; Cholesterol: 190mg; Sodium: 791mg; Fiber: 3g; Sugar: 4g

1. Combine the onion and potatoes in the bottom of the slow cooker.
2. Add the chicken on top.
3. In a small bowl, whisk together the lime juice, orange juice, oil, garlic, salt, oregano, and cumin. Pour the sauce on top of all the ingredients in the slow cooker.
4. Top with the sliced lemon and jalapeño.
5. Cover and cook on low for 5 to 7 hours.

Tip: You can also use a small boneless turkey breast for this dish, or a 2- to 3-pound pork tenderloin.

chicken tikka masala

SERVES 4 / COOK TIME: 5 TO 7 HOURS ON LOW

GLUTEN-FREE • PALEO • DAIRY-FREE

My all-time favorite Indian dish, chicken tikka masala, consists of chunks of chicken cooked in a creamy, spicy, orange-hued curry. While most tikka masala recipes require a lot of steps, this one lets you just throw everything in the slow cooker—but don't worry, this doesn't compromise the flavor. Try to use full-fat coconut milk if you prefer not to use coconut cream; the light variety simply won't achieve the same consistency.

2 pounds boneless, skinless chicken thighs, cut into bite-size pieces

1 (28-ounce) can diced tomatoes, with their juice

1 (15-ounce) can coconut cream or full-fat coconut milk

1 large onion, diced

4 garlic cloves, minced

3 tablespoons tomato paste

2 tablespoons garam masala

2 teaspoons salt

1½ teaspoons paprika

½ teaspoon ground ginger

Chopped fresh cilantro, for garnish

1. Put the chicken in the slow cooker.

2. In a large bowl, combine the vegetables, coconut cream, tomato paste, and seasonings, and mix well. Pour the sauce into the slow cooker and mix to coat the chicken.

3. Cover and cook on low for 5 to 7 hours. Garnish with the cilantro before serving.

Tip: Serve this hearty dish over brown rice or cauliflower rice.

PER SERVING Calories: 600; Total Fat: 38g; Saturated Fat: 27g; Protein: 50g; Carbohydrates: 23g; Cholesterol: 200mg; Sodium: 1,411mg; Fiber: 8g; Sugar: 13g

mediterranean chicken

SERVES 4 / COOK TIME: 5 TO 7 HOURS ON LOW

GLUTEN-FREE • DAIRY-FREE

I first prepared this recipe after returning home from a trip to Greece. I had enjoyed Mediterranean food before, but I really fell in love with it on my visit. The fresh herbs, lemons, and olive oil characteristic of the region are right up my alley. Speaking of herbs, if you have fresh cilantro and oregano, that really makes a difference in this dish.

2 to 3 pounds boneless, skinless chicken thighs

1 (15-ounce) can chickpeas, rinsed and drained

2 pints cherry tomatoes

1 lemon, sliced

4 garlic cloves, minced

2 tablespoons extra-virgin olive oil

1 tablespoon freshly squeezed lemon juice

Handful chopped fresh cilantro

1 teaspoon dried oregano

1 teaspoon paprika

1 teaspoon ground coriander

1 teaspoon ground cumin

1 teaspoon curry powder

1 teaspoon chili pepper

1 teaspoon salt

1. Put the chicken in the slow cooker.

2. In a medium bowl, combine the remaining ingredients and mix well.

3. Pour the mixture over the chicken and stir to coat well.

4. Cover and cook on low for 5 to 7 hours.

Tip: I've made this with every cut of chicken, and while they are all good options, dark meat seems to work best with this recipe.

PER SERVING Calories: 427; Total Fat: 17g; Saturated Fat: 3g; Protein: 49g; Carbohydrates: 21g; Cholesterol: 190mg; Sodium: 907mg; Fiber: 8g; Sugar: 8g

lemon-garlic chicken, potatoes, and asparagus

SERVES 4 / COOK TIME: 5 TO 7 HOURS ON LOW

GLUTEN-FREE • DAIRY-FREE

This recipe can be transformed into several different dishes by substituting various ingredients. For example, you might make it once using red potatoes and green beans; then next time, use sweet potatoes and asparagus. (Yes, you can cook asparagus in the slow cooker without it getting soggy.) The key to this recipe lies in the sauce, which consists of all fresh, natural ingredients. It's nice and light for a healthy meal you can eat any time of day or evening.

2 pounds boneless, skinless chicken thighs

1 pound red potatoes, chopped

1 pound asparagus, trimmed

⅓ cup freshly squeezed lemon juice

¼ cup water

4 garlic cloves, minced

2 teaspoons dried basil

2 teaspoons garlic salt

1 teaspoon salt

1 teaspoon freshly ground black pepper

½ teaspoon red pepper flakes

1 lemon, sliced

1. Combine the chicken, potatoes, and asparagus in the bottom of the slow cooker.

2. In a small bowl, whisk together the lemon juice, water, garlic, basil, garlic salt, salt, black pepper, and red pepper flakes. Pour the sauce over the food in the slow cooker.

3. Top with the lemon slices.

4. Cover and cook on low for 5 to 7 hours.

Tip: Instead of asparagus, you can use green beans, broccoli, carrots, or even kale or spinach.

PER SERVING Calories: 378; Total Fat: 10g; Saturated Fat: 2g; Protein: 49g; Carbohydrates: 25g; Cholesterol: 190mg; Sodium: 796mg; Fiber: 5g; Sugar: 4g

italian chicken with green beans and mushrooms

SERVES 4 / COOK TIME: 5 TO 7 HOURS ON LOW

GLUTEN-FREE • DAIRY-FREE

This is a repeat recipe in my household because of how simple and flavorful it is. Using common Italian ingredients, it's another dish you can jazz up as much as you like with your favorite vegetables. The real key to this recipe's flavor, however, is the Italian seasoning blend. Making your own is so easy, there's no reason to buy it at the store. I keep a huge jar of this homemade mixture in my pantry at all times, as it's delicious on pretty much everything.

FOR THE ITALIAN SEASONING

1 tablespoon dried basil

1 tablespoon dried oregano

1 tablespoon dried rosemary

1 tablespoon dried marjoram

1 tablespoon dried cilantro

1 tablespoon dried thyme

1 tablespoon red pepper flakes

FOR THE CHICKEN

3 cups Marinara Sauce (page 73), or store-bought

2 pounds boneless, skinless chicken thighs

1 pound green beans, trimmed

8 ounces mushrooms, sliced

TO MAKE THE SEASONING

1. Combine all the ingredients in a small food processor.

2. Blend or pulse until the desired consistency is achieved.

3. Store in an airtight container.

TO MAKE THE CHICKEN

1. Pour the marinara sauce into the slow cooker.

2. Place the chicken thighs on top and season them with 2 tablespoons of the Italian seasoning.

3. Add the green beans and mushrooms.

4. Cover and cook on low for 5 to 7 hours.

Tip: Substitute or add whatever vegetables you like best—onions, bell peppers, and eggplant, for example, would all be delicious.

PER SERVING Calories: 430; Total Fat: 9g; Saturated Fat: 3g; Protein: 52g; Carbohydrates: 41g; Cholesterol: 193mg; Sodium: 512mg; Fiber: 9g; Sugar: 15g

citrus-cilantro chicken, potatoes, and summer squash

SERVES 4 / COOK TIME: 5 TO 7 HOURS ON LOW

GLUTEN-FREE • DAIRY-FREE

A light, homemade citrus sauce is added to chicken, potatoes, and your favorite vegetables in this easy one-pot recipe. I nicknamed this my "farmers' market slow cooker meal," because I like to combine my latest market finds, whether carrots, sweet potatoes, baby potatoes, bell peppers, or onions.

FOR THE CHICKEN

1 pound zucchini, chopped

1 pound yellow squash, chopped

1 pound red potatoes, diced

2 pounds boneless, skinless chicken thighs, cut into bite-size pieces

FOR THE SAUCE

¼ cup freshly squeezed lime juice

¼ cup freshly squeezed orange juice

2 tablespoons low-sodium soy sauce, tamari, or coconut aminos

2 tablespoons extra-virgin olive oil

2 teaspoons honey

2 scallions, sliced

2 garlic cloves, minced

½ bunch cilantro, stems removed

1 teaspoon grated lime zest

1 teaspoon grated orange zest

1 teaspoon salt

1. Combine the zucchini, yellow squash, and potatoes in the bottom of the slow cooker.

2. Add the chicken pieces on top.

3. In a small bowl, whisk together all the sauce ingredients. Pour the sauce over the chicken and vegetables.

4. Cover and cook on low for 5 to 7 hours.

Tip: Don't make the mistake of using beets! I did this once and they dyed everything else red. It tasted fine but was not visually appealing at all.

PER SERVING Calories: 465; Total Fat: 17g; Saturated Fat: 3g; Protein: 50g; Carbohydrates: 33g; Cholesterol: 190mg; Sodium: 1,254mg; Fiber: 5g; Sugar: 10g

herbed cornish hens

SERVES 4 / COOK TIME: 5 TO 7 HOURS ON LOW

GLUTEN-FREE • PALEO • DAIRY-FREE

Cornish hens may sound exotic, but they are basically just very young broiler chickens and therefore somewhat smaller. Cornish hens aren't as common as chicken or turkey, but they cook the same way, especially in the slow cooker. My large 6-quart slow cooker fits two Cornish hens comfortably, but fitting in the rest of the ingredients can be tight. So be conscious of the size of your cooker when buying the hens. Depending on the size of the hens, a single one can feed either one or two people.

¼ cup low-sodium chicken broth

2 Cornish hens

1 teaspoon poultry seasoning

1 teaspoon salt

½ teaspoon freshly ground black pepper

1 cup cherry tomatoes

8 ounces green beans, trimmed

8 ounces sweet potatoes, peeled and chopped

....

PER SERVING Calories: 263; Total Fat: 12g; Saturated Fat: 3g; Protein: 17g; Carbohydrates: 22g; Cholesterol: 85mg; Sodium: 648mg; Fiber: 5g; Sugar: 2g

1. Pour the broth into the slow cooker.
2. Season the Cornish hens with the poultry seasoning, salt, and pepper, and place them side by side in the slow cooker.
3. Nestle the vegetables around the hens.
4. Cover and cook on low for 5 to 7 hours.

Tip: Chopped butternut squash would offer a tasty alternative to the sweet potatoes.

jerk chicken with corn and black beans

SERVES 4 / COOK TIME: 5 TO 7 HOURS ON LOW

GLUTEN-FREE • DAIRY-FREE

We commonly associate Jamaican food with intense flavor, but it's also known for its use of fresh, wholesome ingredients. This recipe is a good example of that—with a heavenly aroma to prove it.

FOR THE CHICKEN

2½ pounds boneless, skinless chicken thighs, cut into bite-size pieces

2 red or green bell peppers, seeded and sliced

1 red onion, sliced

1 (15-ounce) can corn, drained

1 (15-ounce) can black beans, rinsed and drained

FOR THE SAUCE

½ cup water

¼ cup honey

2 tablespoons extra-virgin olive oil

3 garlic cloves, minced

1½ teaspoons salt

½ teaspoon red pepper flakes

½ teaspoon ground cumin

½ teaspoon ground cinnamon

....

PER SERVING Calories: 600; Total Fat: 19g; Saturated Fat: 4g; Protein: 64g; Carbohydrates: 50g; Cholesterol: 235mg; Sodium: 3,542mg; Fiber: 8g; Sugar: 25g

1. Combine the chicken, bell peppers, onion, corn, and black beans in the slow cooker and mix well.

2. In a medium bowl, whisk together all the sauce ingredients. Pour the sauce into the slow cooker and stir to make sure all the chicken and vegetables are coated.

3. Cover and cook on low for 5 to 7 hours.

Tip: Freezer meal alert! Bag this one up and pop it in the freezer for later use. Add a minced serrano chile if you're looking to increase the heat.

greek chicken with potatoes, green beans, and olives

SERVES 4 / COOK TIME: 5 TO 7 HOURS ON LOW

GLUTEN-FREE • DAIRY-FREE

One of the best things about Greek cuisine is that it features lots of light, fresh ingredients like lemons and extra-virgin olive oil. I tried to keep the sauce for this dish along those lines, based on water, vinegar, and lemon. Use fresh oregano if you can—it's not required but will intensify the level of flavor.

FOR THE CHICKEN

2 pounds boneless, skinless chicken thighs, cut into bite-size pieces

2 pounds red potatoes, cut in half

½ red onion, sliced

1 pound green beans, trimmed

1 cup cherry tomatoes

¼ cup pitted Kalamata olives

FOR THE SAUCE

⅓ cup water

⅓ cup freshly squeezed lemon juice

¼ cup red wine vinegar

2 teaspoons extra-virgin olive oil

3 garlic cloves, minced

2 teaspoons dried oregano

½ teaspoon salt

¼ teaspoon freshly ground black pepper

1. Combine the chicken, potatoes, onion, green beans, tomatoes, and olives in the slow cooker.

2. In a medium bowl, whisk together all the sauce ingredients. Pour the sauce into the slow cooker, and stir to make sure all the chicken and vegetables are coated.

3. Cover and cook on low for 5 to 7 hours.

Tip: You don't have to use red potatoes here—use whatever variety you have available. Just try to chop the potatoes in equal-size pieces so they cook evenly.

PER SERVING Calories: 511; Total Fat: 13g; Saturated Fat: 3g; Protein: 51g; Carbohydrates: 50g; Cholesterol: 190mg; Sodium: 592mg; Fiber: 9g; Sugar: 6g

sweet and spicy chicken

SERVES 4 / COOK TIME: 5 TO 7 HOURS ON LOW

GLUTEN-FREE • DAIRY-FREE

This recipe should really be titled "a little bit of sweet and a lot of spice." If you're not a big fan of spicy, I suggest reducing the amount of sriracha to create a milder sauce. This sauce can be used for vegetarian meals as well—simply omit the chicken thighs and add more potatoes or more vegetables like carrots or green beans.

FOR THE CHICKEN

2 pounds boneless, skinless chicken thighs

1 pound red potatoes, quartered

2 red or green bell peppers, seeded and chopped

1 onion, chopped

FOR THE SAUCE

¾ cup honey

½ cup sriracha

¼ cup low-sodium soy sauce, tamari, or coconut aminos

2 garlic cloves, minced

2 teaspoons dried basil

....

PER SERVING Calories: 600; Total Fat: 9g; Saturated Fat: 2g; Protein: 49g; Carbohydrates: 80g; Cholesterol: 190mg; Sodium: 1,319mg; Fiber: 4g; Sugar: 59g

1. Combine the chicken thighs, potatoes, bell peppers, and onion in the slow cooker.

2. In a medium bowl, whisk together all the sauce ingredients. Pour the sauce into the slow cooker, and stir to make sure all the chicken and vegetables are coated.

3. Cover and cook on low for 5 to 7 hours.

Tip: The chicken will be very tender when it's done cooking. You can shred the thighs or leave them whole. This makes a delicious meal served over brown rice, cauliflower rice, quinoa, or couscous.

latin chicken with black beans and peppers

SERVES 4 / COOK TIME: 5 TO 7 HOURS ON LOW

GLUTEN-FREE • DAIRY-FREE

This recipe gives you lots of options for the finished dish. Most often I eat it as is, but the chicken is also great stuffed into a tortilla, shredded over lettuce, or served with brown rice or quinoa for a burrito bowl. You can even throw in some diced sweet potatoes prior to cooking to create a more complete meal.

1 cup salsa

1 (15-ounce) can black beans, rinsed and drained

2 red or green bell peppers, seeded and sliced

1 onion, sliced

2 pounds boneless, skinless chicken thighs, cut into bite-size pieces

1 or 2 jalapeños, minced

1 garlic clove, minced

¼ cup chopped fresh cilantro

2 teaspoons ground cumin

1 teaspoon paprika

1. Combine the salsa, black beans, bell peppers, and onion in the slow cooker and mix well.

2. Add the chicken, jalapeños, cilantro, cumin, and paprika, and stir to combine.

3. Cover and cook on low for 5 to 7 hours.

Tip: Instead of jalapeños, you can use canned chipotles in adobo sauce. Tired of chicken? Use beef or pork instead!

. . . .

PER SERVING Calories: 371; Total Fat: 10g; Saturated Fat: 2g; Protein: 51g; Carbohydrates: 22g; Cholesterol: 190mg; Sodium: 674mg; Fiber: 7g; Sugar: 8g

honey-garlic chicken

SERVES 4 / COOK TIME: 5 TO 7 HOURS ON LOW

GLUTEN-FREE • DAIRY-FREE

Honey and garlic are two of my favorite natural ingredients to pair in a slow cooker sauce—the honey coats the meat, while the garlic adds flavor. This is yet another recipe that works with pretty much any cut of chicken—I like to use thighs, as dark meat prepared in this way always tastes great. You can even use a whole chicken.

FOR THE CHICKEN

1½ pounds red potatoes, halved

1 pounds green beans, trimmed

2 pounds chicken boneless, skinless chicken thighs

FOR THE SAUCE

½ cup low-sodium soy sauce, tamari, or coconut aminos

½ cup honey

2 tablespoons Ketchup (page 122)

2 tablespoons sriracha

4 garlic cloves, minced

1 teaspoon dried basil

½ teaspoon dried oregano

¼ teaspoon freshly ground black pepper

1. Combine the potatoes and green beans in the slow cooker.

2. Add the chicken on top.

3. In a small bowl, whisk together all the sauce ingredients. Pour the sauce on top of the chicken and vegetables.

4. Cover and cook on low for 5 to 7 hours.

Tip: To make this a Paleo meal, replace the potatoes with 1½ pounds of chopped sweet potatoes, pumpkin, or butternut squash.

PER SERVING Calories: 583; Total Fat: 10g; Saturated Fat: 2g; Protein: 52g; Carbohydrates: 79g; Cholesterol: 190mg; Sodium: 2,116mg; Fiber: 7g; Sugar: 42g

paleo butter chicken

SERVES 4 / COOK TIME: 5 TO 7 HOURS ON LOW

GLUTEN-FREE • PALEO

This recipe is another Indian-inspired dish. This Paleo version succeeds in being healthy without compromising the flavors of butter chicken we all love so much. Butter chicken is usually cooked in a tandoori oven, but unfortunately that can overcook the meat and dry it out. This slow cooker version produces an especially moist and succulent dish every time.

2 pounds boneless, skinless chicken thighs

1 (15-ounce) can coconut cream or full-fat coconut milk

1 onion, diced

1 (6-ounce) can tomato paste

1½ teaspoons ghee

3 tablespoons freshly squeezed lime juice

3 garlic cloves, minced

2 teaspoons ground cumin

1 teaspoon ground ginger

1 teaspoon ground coriander

1 teaspoon curry powder

1 teaspoon salt

¼ cup chopped fresh cilantro, for garnish

1. Combine all the ingredients except the cilantro in the slow cooker and mix well.

2. Cover and cook on low for 5 to 7 hours.

3. Garnish with the fresh cilantro before serving.

Tip: The chicken will be very tender when it's done. You can shred it or leave it whole. Serve over rice or with whole-wheat naan.

PER SERVING Calories: 465; Total Fat: 24g; Saturated Fat: 16g; Protein: 49g; Carbohydrates: 15g; Cholesterol: 194mg; Sodium: 839mg; Fiber: 3g; Sugar: 7g

rotisserie turkey legs

SERVES 4 / COOK TIME: 5 TO 7 HOURS ON LOW

GLUTEN-FREE • PALEO • DAIRY-FREE

Every time I go to Disneyland, I have to get one of those big turkey legs, so this recipe is my ode to the Disneyland turkey leg. The appropriate size slow cooker to use will depend on how much meat you have. Four medium-size turkey legs should fit in a 6-quart oval model. I choose to put the legs on top of a wire rack so the grease will drip to the bottom of the cooker, rather than let the food cook in it. If you don't have a rack, you can ball up some aluminum foil, or even put the legs on top of a chopped-up onion. Alternatively, there is absolutely nothing wrong with having the meat cook directly in the bottom of the slow cooker; just add ¼ cup of water or low-sodium broth.

2 tablespoons extra-virgin olive oil

4 medium turkey legs
   (about 3 pounds total)

1 tablespoon paprika

1 tablespoon garlic powder

1 tablespoon oregano

2 teaspoons salt

2 teaspoons freshly ground
   black pepper

1. Rub the oil evenly over the turkey legs.

2. Stir the seasonings together in a small bowl, and rub them generously on each turkey leg.

3. Place the turkey legs in the slow cooker.

4. Cover and cook on low for 5 to 7 hours.

Tip: If you have your own homemade rotisserie seasoning blend, by all means use that. If you can't find turkey legs, just substitute 3 pounds of chicken legs.

PER SERVING Calories: 380; Total Fat: 21g; Saturated Fat: 5g; Protein: 43g; Carbohydrates: 4g; Cholesterol: 163mg; Sodium: 1,329mg; Fiber: 2g; Sugar: 1g

spicy turkey sausage and vegetables

SERVES 4 / COOK TIME: 5 TO 7 HOURS ON LOW

GLUTEN-FREE • PALEO • DAIRY-FREE

This is one of my favorite recipes: Not only is this dish "throw it all in and go," but it's also Paleo, gluten-free and low-calorie. You can make it even healthier by loading it up with more vegetables, like zucchini, celery, or carrots. The paprika and red pepper flakes bring on the heat, so reduce the amount of these two seasonings or omit them altogether if you prefer a less spicy dish.

2 ¼ pounds fully cooked turkey sausage links, cut into 1-inch pieces

½ cup low-sodium chicken broth

2 red or green bell peppers, seeded and chopped

1 celery stalk, chopped

1 medium onion, chopped

3 Roma tomatoes, diced

1 bay leaf

1 tablespoon paprika

2 teaspoons dried thyme

1 teaspoon red pepper flakes

1 teaspoon garlic powder

1. Combine all the ingredients in the slow cooker and mix well.

2. Cover and cook on low 5 to 7 hours.

3. Remove the bay leaf before serving.

Tip: For a more complete meal, stir in 2 cups of cooked brown rice or quinoa once the dish has completed cooking.

PER SERVING Calories: 472; Total Fat: 20g; Saturated Fat: 6g; Protein: 60g; Carbohydrates: 13g; Cholesterol: 150mg; Sodium: 1,033mg; Fiber: 4g; Sugar: 7g

herbed turkey breast

SERVES 6 / COOK TIME: 5 TO 7 HOURS ON LOW

GLUTEN-FREE • DAIRY-FREE

This recipe reminds me that slow cooking doesn't have to be fancy or complicated. With just simple herbs and a little bit of broth, the result is extremely succulent turkey. Please note this recipe uses turkey breast, not a whole turkey. (I've yet to find a whole turkey that will fit in my slow cooker, even my largest one!) Bone-in or boneless doesn't matter; the finished meat will be so tender it should fall apart when you remove it from the slow cooker.

½ cup low-sodium chicken broth

1 tablespoon extra-virgin olive oil

1 (3- to 4-pound) bone-in, skin-on turkey breast

3 garlic cloves, minced

1 teaspoon salt

½ teaspoon dried thyme

½ teaspoon dried rosemary

½ teaspoon dried sage

¼ teaspoon freshly ground black pepper

1½ pounds red potatoes, halved

1 pound green beans or asparagus, trimmed

1. Pour the broth into the slow cooker.

2. Rub the oil all over the turkey breast.

3. Season the turkey breast with the garlic and seasonings, and place it in the slow cooker.

4. Nestle the potatoes and green beans around the turkey breast.

5. Cover and cook on low for 5 to 7 hours.

Tip: If you like, swap in different herbs, like oregano or basil. Or for a bit of spiciness, add ½ teaspoon of paprika.

PER SERVING Calories: 558; Total Fat: 19g; Saturated Fat: 5g; Protein: 53g; Carbohydrates: 35g; Cholesterol: 140mg; Sodium: 686mg; Fiber: 6g; Sugar: 3g

turkey breast of wonder

SERVES 6 / COOK TIME: 5 TO 7 HOURS ON LOW

GLUTEN-FREE • PALEO • DAIRY-FREE

This is not my original recipe—the author is unknown—but this *is* my slow cooker version. I made it healthier by using all natural ingredients like extra-virgin olive oil, fresh cranberries (rather than canned), fresh orange juice, and seasonings. And despite the title, you can just as easily use any combo of up to 5 pounds turkey legs, wings, or other parts. Just keep in mind that dark meat takes an hour or so more to cook, so check the temperature to ensure your turkey is fully cooked before serving.

1 (3- to 4-pound) bone-in, skin-on turkey breast

½ cup freshly squeezed orange juice

1 tablespoon extra-virgin olive oil

3 tablespoons dried minced onion

1 teaspoon dried parsley

½ teaspoon onion powder

½ teaspoon ground turmeric

½ teaspoon salt

¼ teaspoon freshly ground black pepper

¼ teaspoon celery salt

⅛ teaspoon garlic powder

10 ounces fresh cranberries

1. Place the turkey breast in the slow cooker.

2. In a small bowl, whisk together the orange juice, olive oil, and seasonings. Pour the sauce over the turkey.

3. Top with the fresh cranberries.

4. Cover and cook on low for 5 to 7 hours.

Tip: Don't overcook the turkey! White meat in particular will easily overcook if left in the slow cooker too long, even on the warm setting.

PER SERVING Calories: 439; Total Fat: 18g; Saturated Fat: 4g; Protein: 48g; Carbohydrates: 7g; Cholesterol: 140mg; Sodium: 475mg; Fiber: 2g; Sugar: 4g

louisiana creole turkey

SERVES 4 / COOK TIME: 5 TO 7 HOURS ON LOW

GLUTEN-FREE • DAIRY-FREE

Creole seasonings add a spicy note to this healthy turkey recipe. It's perfect for a turkey with a twist at your next Thanksgiving, or if you're just looking to add something new and different to a family dinner at any time of year. This recipe includes a pound of potatoes and a whole bunch of veggies, so it's a complete one-pot meal.

FOR THE TURKEY

1 pound red potatoes, quartered

1 onion, chopped

2 celery stalks, chopped

1 red or green bell pepper, seeded and chopped

2 carrots, peeled and chopped

1 (3- to 4-pound) boneless, skinless turkey breast

FOR THE SAUCE

½ cup low-sodium broth

1 tablespoon freshly squeezed lemon juice

2 garlic cloves, minced

1 tablespoon garlic powder

2 teaspoons paprika

1½ teaspoons salt

1½ teaspoons onion powder

1½ teaspoons dried oregano

1½ teaspoons dried thyme

1 teaspoon cayenne pepper

1 teaspoon freshly ground black pepper

1. Combine the potatoes and vegetables in the slow cooker.

2. Place the turkey breast on top.

3. In a small bowl, whisk together all the sauce ingredients. Pour the sauce into the slow cooker, making sure it coats the turkey and vegetables.

4. Cover and cook on low for 5 to 7 hours.

....

PER SERVING Calories: 513; Total Fat: 2g; Saturated Fat: 0g; Protein: 89g; Carbohydrates: 34g; Cholesterol: 135mg; Sodium: 3,610mg; Fiber: 6g; Sugar: 8g

Tip: To make this meal Paleo compliant, replace the potatoes with sweet potatoes or even butternut squash.

Lamb and Apricot Tagine with Chickpeas *page 139*

pork, beef, and lamb

....

salsa verde pork

SERVES 4 / COOK TIME: 8 TO 10 HOURS ON LOW

GLUTEN-FREE • PALEO • DAIRY-FREE

Salsa verde is a green salsa made with natural ingredients. Combine this salsa with pork (or chicken) for a quick and healthy slow cooker recipe that is sure to please. You can use this brightly flavored meat in so many ways: in enchiladas, in a salad, or of course to make tacos. You'll know the pork is fully cooked when it shreds easily with two forks. If you take it out and it doesn't shred easily, just put it back in the slow cooker and let it cook for another 30 minutes.

FOR THE PORK

1 (2-pound) pork tenderloin

1 small onion, sliced

FOR THE SALSA VERDE

½ pound tomatillos, husks removed

½ jalapeño, seeded and
    roughly chopped

½ onion, roughly chopped

1 garlic clove, peeled

2 tablespoons chopped fresh cilantro

1 tablespoon freshly squeezed
    lime juice

¼ teaspoon extra-virgin olive oil

½ teaspoon salt

1. Put the pork loin and onion in the slow cooker.

2. Combine all the salsa ingredients in a food processor and pulse until the desired consistency is achieved.

3. Pour the salsa on top of the pork.

4. Cover and cook on low for 8 to 10 hours.

Tip: If you have time, roast the tomatillos, jalapeño, onion, and garlic in the oven at 400°F for 15 to 20 minutes, or until nicely charred, before adding them to the food processor.

....

PER SERVING Calories: 316; Total Fat: 9g; Saturated Fat: 3g; Protein: 47g; Carbohydrates: 7g; Cholesterol: 150mg; Sodium: 413mg; Fiber: 2g; Sugar: 2g

sweet and tangy pork tenderloin

SERVES 6 / COOK TIME: 8 TO 10 HOURS ON LOW

GLUTEN-FREE • DAIRY-FREE

The star of this recipe is the sweet and tangy sauce, which uses healthy, natural ingredients. Honey and cinnamon together have great benefits, like the ability to control inflammation and boost the immune system. As always, taste the sauce while you're making it! If you think it needs to be sweeter, add more honey. Needs a little more tang? Add more vinegar.

FOR THE PORK

1½ pounds red potatoes, quartered

1 small red onion, sliced

1 (3-pound) pork tenderloin

FOR THE SAUCE

¼ cup water

¼ cup apple cider vinegar

¼ cup honey

1 tablespoon ground cinnamon

¼ teaspoon salt

⅛ teaspoon freshly ground
  black pepper

⅓ cup pomegranate seeds

1. Combine the potatoes and onion in the slow cooker.

2. Place the pork tenderloin on top.

3. In a small bowl, whisk together all the sauce ingredients. Pour the sauce over the tenderloin.

4. Top with the pomegranate seeds.

5. Cover and cook on low for 8 to 10 hours.

Tip: For a complete meal, add a few chopped root vegetables in the bottom of the slow cooker along with the potatoes and onion.

PER SERVING Calories: 438; Total Fat: 5g; Saturated Fat: 2g; Protein: 52g; Carbohydrates: 47g; Cholesterol: 150mg; Sodium: 260mg; Fiber: 4g; Sugar: 16g

country ribs and sauerkraut

SERVES 4 / COOK TIME: 8 TO 10 HOURS ON LOW

GLUTEN-FREE • PALEO • DAIRY-FREE

"Kraut and ribs" is what I like to call this. For the ribs, country-style works best, but you can use baby backs or any other type of ribs, or even pork chops. You might have to cut the recipe in half depending on the size of your slow cooker. For a unique spin, try serving this on a whole-wheat bun for a hearty kraut and rib sandwich.

3¾ pounds boneless country-style pork ribs

2 garlic cloves, minced

1 onion, sliced

1 (32-ounce) jar sauerkraut, rinsed and drained

2 tablespoons honey

1½ teaspoons dried thyme

....

PER SERVING Calories: 599; Total Fat: 17g; Saturated Fat: 7g; Protein: 94g; Carbohydrates: 22g; Cholesterol: 201mg; Sodium: 2,323mg; Fiber: 7g; Sugar: 14g

1. Combine the ribs, garlic, and onion in the slow cooker.

2. Spread the sauerkraut on top.

3. Drizzle with the honey and then sprinkle with the thyme.

4. Cover and cook on low for 8 to 10 hours.

Tip: Add 1 or 2 diced potatoes to the bottom of the slow cooker along with the ribs, garlic, and onion for a well-rounded meal. Don't have thyme? Use rosemary!

apple-dijon kielbasa, sauerkraut, and potatoes

SERVES 4 / COOK TIME: 8 TO 10 HOURS ON LOW

GLUTEN-FREE • DAIRY-FREE

I grew up eating a lot of kielbasa and sauerkraut. No, I'm not Polish, but this dish was on regular rotation in my household because it not only is extremely easy to make, but also uses fairly cheap ingredients. I encourage you to read the labels when buying a kielbasa or sausage. Try to find one that's low-sodium and contains no added sugar. The liquid smoke is optional for exactly that: a touch of smokiness.

1 apple, peeled, cored, and diced

1¾ pounds lean turkey kielbasa, cut into 1-inch pieces

1½ pounds new potatoes, cut into 1-inch pieces

1 (32-ounce) jar sauerkraut, rinsed and drained

1 small onion, diced

2 tablespoons Dijon mustard

2 teaspoons dried dill seed

¼ teaspoon liquid smoke (optional)

. . . .

PER SERVING Calories: 555; Total Fat: 15g; Saturated Fat: 4g; Protein: 33g; Carbohydrates: 58g; Cholesterol: 100mg; Sodium: 3,519mg; Fiber: 13g; Sugar: 13g

1. Combine all the ingredients in the slow cooker and mix well.

2. Cover and cook on low for 8 to 10 hours.

> **Tip:** If you have the time, grill the onion before adding it to the slow cooker for an extra hit of flavor.

pulled pork sandwiches with sweet and spicy slaw

SERVES 8 / COOK TIME: 8 TO 10 HOURS ON LOW

GLUTEN-FREE • DAIRY-FREE

Pulled pork is consistently one of the top-searched slow cooker recipes. In a lot of ways, it represents what slow cookers do best: using a cheaper cut of meat and just a few simple ingredients, cooking low and slow all day, and producing the most tender meat that shreds with a fork. And pulled pork can be used so many ways. My favorite is to make pulled pork sandwiches, but it's also great in salads and enchiladas. You can even freeze the cooked meat for later use.

FOR THE SLAW

2 tablespoons freshly squeezed lime juice

2 tablespoons honey

1 tablespoon distilled white vinegar

1 tablespoon extra-virgin olive oil

¼ teaspoon sriracha

½ teaspoon ground cumin

½ teaspoon salt

1 (14-ounce) bag coleslaw blend

¼ cup chopped fresh cilantro

FOR THE PORK SANDWICHES

2 onions, chopped

4 garlic cloves, roughly chopped

2 teaspoons ground cumin

2 teaspoons dried oregano

1½ teaspoons chili powder

1½ teaspoons paprika

1 teaspoon garlic powder

1 teaspoon salt

1 teaspoon cayenne pepper

½ teaspoon freshly ground black pepper

½ teaspoon red pepper flakes

1 (4- to 5-pound) pork shoulder

½ cup water

¼ cup apple cider vinegar

10 whole-wheat or gluten-free hamburger buns

. . . .

PER SERVING Calories: 580; Total Fat: 40g; Saturated Fat: 15g; Protein: 40g; Carbohydrates: 14g; Cholesterol: 140mg; Sodium: 704mg; Fiber: 2g; Sugar: 9g

TO MAKE THE SLAW

1. In a medium bowl, whisk together the lime juice, honey, vinegar, olive oil, sriracha, cumin, and salt.

2. Add the coleslaw blend and cilantro, and mix until everything is completely coated.

3. Cover and refrigerate until ready to serve.

TO MAKE THE PORK SANDWICHES

1. Combine the chopped onions and garlic in the bottom of the slow cooker.

2. Combine the dry seasonings and spread them completely all over the pork. Place the pork on top of the onion.

3. Pour the water and apple cider vinegar over the pork.

4. Cover and cook on low for 8 to 10 hours

5. Remove the pork from the slow cooker and shred it with two forks. Return the shredded meat to the slow cooker and mix it into the sauce.

6. To serve, top each bun with ¼ cup meat and 2 tablespoons slaw.

Tip: Pork butt is another name for pork shoulder; if you can't find it, use boneless country-style ribs.

paleo meatball onion bombs

SERVES 6 / COOK TIME: 8 TO 10 HOURS ON LOW

GLUTEN-FREE • PALEO • DAIRY-FREE

This is a campfire classic converted to a slow cooker recipe. For the meatballs, use the meat of your choice. I suggest either ground beef or pork; ground poultry is an option, but it may dry out too quickly. The homemade ketchup is not required but highly recommended. You can even add it during the last 30 minutes of cook time so it blends better with the other ingredients.

FOR THE MEATBALL ONION BOMBS

6 large yellow onions

2 pounds extra-lean ground
   pork or beef

1 (8-ounce) can tomato sauce

½ cup unsweetened almond milk

1 large egg, lightly beaten

1 cup almond flour

1 small yellow onion, finely chopped

3 garlic cloves, minced

3 tablespoons Italian Seasoning
   (page 100)

1 teaspoon salt

¼ teaspoon freshly ground
   black pepper

¼ cup low-sodium beef broth
   or water

FOR THE KETCHUP

1 (8-ounce) can tomato sauce

½ teaspoon distilled white vinegar

1 teaspoon Italian Seasoning
   (page 100)

....

PER SERVING Calories: 394; Total Fat: 19g; Saturated Fat: 7g; Protein: 36g; Carbohydrates: 20g; Cholesterol: 113mg; Sodium: 915mg; Fiber: 5g; Sugar: 10g

1. Slice off the top and bottom of each onion and peel off the papery skins. Cut each onion in half lengthwise and gently separate the layers.

2. In a large bowl, mix the ground meat, tomato sauce, almond milk, egg, almond flour, chopped onion, garlic, Italian seasoning, salt, and pepper until well combined.

3. Form the meat mixture into 18 meatballs.

4. Place each meatball on a curved piece of onion that fits it nicely, selecting onion pieces that are neither too small nor too large, and secure with toothpicks. (Reserve the leftover onion pieces for another use.)

5. Pour the broth into the slow cooker.

6. Place the onion bombs in a single layer in the bottom of the slow cooker.

7. Cover and cook on low for 8 to 10 hours.

8. In a small bowl, whisk together the ketchup ingredients.

9. Remove the toothpicks from the onion bombs and top them with homemade ketchup before serving.

Tip: Instead of ketchup, feel free to use your favorite homemade or store-bought barbecue sauce. If you're using store-bought, watch out for added sugar.

barbecue baby back ribs and potatoes

SERVES 5 / COOK TIME: 10 TO 12 HOURS ON LOW

GLUTEN-FREE • DAIRY-FREE

If you thought that only a smoker could produce melt-in-your-mouth ribs, just wait until you try them in the slow cooker. You can easily double this recipe and use 5 pounds of ribs. To do so, stand the other rack on the opposite side of the slow cooker to create a ring around the potatoes and onions; it's okay if they overlap a bit. You'll know the meat is ready to serve when it actually falls off the bone.

FOR THE BARBECUE SAUCE

1 (15-ounce) can tomato sauce

1 (6-ounce) can tomato paste

1 cup freshly squeezed orange juice

⅓ cup balsamic vinegar

1 tablespoon low-sodium soy sauce, tamari, or coconut aminos

1 tablespoon honey

¼ teaspoon liquid smoke

1 small onion, minced

3 garlic cloves, minced

1½ teaspoons ground mustard

1 teaspoon ground cumin

1 teaspoon chili powder

1 teaspoon salt

½ teaspoon freshly ground black pepper

½ teaspoon dried basil

FOR THE RIBS

1 (2-pound) rack baby back ribs

1½ teaspoons garlic powder

1½ teaspoons salt

1 teaspoon freshly ground black pepper

½ teaspoon paprika

1 pound red potatoes, cut in half

1 onion, chopped

....

PER SERVING Calories: 580; Total Fat: 35g; Saturated Fat: 13g; Protein: 30g; Carbohydrates: 43g; Cholesterol: 108mg; Sodium: 1,936mg; Fiber: 6g; Sugar: 18g

TO MAKE THE BARBECUE SAUCE

1. Combine all the ingredients in the slow cooker and mix well.

2. Cover and cook on low for low 2 to 4 hours.

3. Blend the sauce with an immersion blender until smooth (or transfer to a food processor and blend). You will need 1 cup of sauce for the ribs; store the remainder in an airtight container in the refrigerator for up to 6 weeks.

TO MAKE THE RIBS

1. Season the ribs all over with the garlic powder, salt, pepper, and paprika.

2. Place the rack in the slow cooker, standing up, with the meaty side facing out.

3. Add the potatoes and onion to the slow cooker inside the ring of standing ribs.

4. Cover and cook on low for 4 hours.

5. Pour 1 cup of the homemade barbecue sauce over the ribs.

6. Re-cover and cook on low for 4 hours.

Tip: If it's not convenient to put the sauce on the ribs halfway through cooking, go ahead and slather it on at the beginning and let it cook on the meat for the entire 8 hours. I recommend you broil the ribs after they're done cooking for few minutes to crisp up the edges. Serve with your favorite barbecue sides.

creamy paleo herbed pork chops

SERVES 4 / COOK TIME: 8 TO 10 HOURS ON LOW

GLUTEN-FREE • PALEO

The word "creamy" in slow cooker recipes usually means that the dish is loaded with butter, heavy cream, or flour. The truth is you don't need any of that to create a slow-cooked creamy sauce—just some creativity. This recipe consists of pork, potatoes, herbs, and a few other healthy ingredients. The creaminess of this dish comes from what's known as a "slurry" of arrowroot powder and water added at the end.

FOR THE PORK

1 onion, sliced

1 red or green bell pepper, seeded and sliced

1 pound sweet potatoes, peeled and diced

2 pounds bone-in pork chops

FOR THE SAUCE

1½ cups low-sodium chicken broth

4 garlic cloves, minced

1 tablespoon ghee, melted

1 teaspoon dried parsley

1 teaspoon dried oregano

1 teaspoon dried basil

1 teaspoon dried thyme

1 teaspoon salt

½ teaspoon freshly ground black pepper

FOR THE SLURRY

2 tablespoons arrowroot powder

¼ cup cold water

1. Combine the onion, bell pepper, and sweet potatoes in the slow cooker.

2. Place the pork chops on top.

3. In a small bowl, whisk together all the sauce ingredients.

4. Pour the sauce into the slow cooker, making sure that all the ingredients are covered.

5. Cover and cook on low for 8 to 10 hours.

6. During the last 20 minutes of cook time, whisk together the arrowroot and water. Pour the slurry into the slow cooker, stir, re-cover, and finish cooking to thicken the sauce.

....

PER SERVING Calories: 599; Total Fat: 30g; Saturated Fat: 11g; Protein: 56g; Carbohydrates: 39g; Cholesterol: 108mg; Sodium: 720mg; Fiber: 6g; Sugar: 4g

Tip: Arrowroot is natural starch. If you can't find it, you can substitute cornstarch.

campfire pot

SERVES 4 / COOK TIME: 8 TO 10 HOURS ON LOW

GLUTEN-FREE • DAIRY-FREE

This was my first meal on my first camping trip. Thirty years later, I still remember this recipe like it was yesterday. I made a few modifications to convert it for the slow cooker, but for the most part, the recipe remains unchanged. It uses simple ingredients like ground meat and fresh vegetables. And just as at a campfire, it cooks in aluminum foil.

1½ pounds extra lean
    ground pork (99%)

1 pound bacon, chopped (optional)

¾ pound red potatoes, diced

1 onion, diced

2 red or green bell peppers,
    seeded and diced

3 carrots, peeled and diced

1 teaspoon garlic powder

1 teaspoon ground cumin

1 teaspoon dried rosemary

1 teaspoon salt

1 teaspoon freshly ground
    black pepper

1. In a large bowl, combine all the ingredients until they are well mixed.

2. Lay out a large sheet of aluminum foil. Transfer the meat and vegetable mixture to the foil and fold over the edges to create a sealed packet.

3. Place the packet in the bottom of the slow cooker.

4. Cover and cook on low 8 to 10 hours, or until the potatoes are tender. (Note: The foil will become extremely hot, so use oven mitts when removing the packet from the slow cooker.)

Tip: The bacon does not need to be precooked. If you choose to use ground poultry, reduce the cook time to 5 to 7 hours.

PER SERVING Calories: 598; Total Fat: 32g; Saturated Fat: 12g; Protein: 44g; Carbohydrates: 29g; Cholesterol: 159mg; Sodium: 1,211mg; Fiber: 5g; Sugar: 8g

steak fajitas

SERVES 4 / COOK TIME: 8 TO 10 HOURS ON LOW

GLUTEN-FREE • PALEO • DAIRY-FREE

While slow cooker fajitas may not give you the "sizzle" of skillet fajitas, they sure make up for it in flavor—and convenience. My seasoning recipe makes about 2½ tablespoons, which is equivalent to one packet of the store-bought kind. I make a big batch and keep it in a Mason jar in my cupboard. Using this homemade seasoning versus a store-bought fajita packet will reduce the sodium intake of this meal by a whopping 50 percent.

FOR THE FAJITA SEASONING

1 tablespoon chili powder

1½ teaspoons ground cumin

1 teaspoon salt

1 teaspoon freshly ground
   black pepper

½ teaspoon dried oregano

½ teaspoon paprika

¼ teaspoon garlic powder

¼ teaspoon onion powder

¼ teaspoon red pepper flakes

FOR THE STEAK

2½ cups salsa of your choice

2 pounds boneless rump roast,
   cut into thin strips

1 onion, sliced

2 red or green bell peppers,
   seeded and sliced

1. In a small bowl, combine all the ingredients for the fajita seasoning.

2. Pour the salsa into the slow cooker.

3. Add the beef, onion, bell peppers, and fajita seasoning. Stir to mix well.

4. Cover and cook on low for 8 to 10 hours.

Tip: There are so many ways to serve this: with whole-wheat tortillas, over brown rice, or in a steak salad are just a few suggestions.

PER SERVING Calories: 385; Total Fat: 13g;
Saturated Fat: 4g; Protein: 53g;
Carbohydrates: 14g; Cholesterol: 150mg;
Sodium: 1,222mg; Fiber: 4g; Sugar: 7g

low-carb paleo cabbage rolls

SERVES 4 / COOK TIME: 8 TO 10 HOURS ON LOW

GLUTEN-FREE • PALEO • DAIRY-FREE

While cabbage rolls might not be the first thing that comes to mind when you think of a light and easy slow cooker recipe, this is one of the healthiest dishes in this cookbook. To create a low-carb version, I replaced the rice with uncooked cauliflower "rice." Cauliflower rice is simply a head of cauliflower that is pulsed in the food processor until it resembles rice.

1 pound extra-lean ground beef

2 cups cauliflower rice
   (about 1 small head)

1 small onion, diced

3 garlic cloves, minced

2 teaspoons Italian Seasoning
   (page 100) or dried oregano

1 teaspoon salt

¼ teaspoon freshly ground
   black pepper

1 head cabbage, cored,
   leaves separated

1 (15-ounce) can diced tomatoes,
   with their juice

. . . .

PER SERVING Calories: 238; Total Fat: 8g; Saturated Fat: 3g; Protein: 21g; Carbohydrates: 23g; Cholesterol: 41mg; Sodium: 697mg; Fiber: 9g; Sugar: 12g

1. In a large bowl, mix the ground beef, cauliflower rice, onion, garlic, Italian seasoning, salt, and pepper.

2. Place the cabbage leaves on a plate and microwave for 15 to 30 seconds, or until warm and pliable.

3. Fill each leaf with about ¼ cup of the meat-cauliflower mixture. Roll up the leaf like a burrito.

4. Spoon a thin layer of diced tomatoes in the bottom of the slow cooker.

5. Add the cabbage rolls, seam-side down.

6. Pour the rest of the diced tomatoes and their juice on top.

7. Cover and cook on low for 8 to 10 hours.

Tip: If you prefer, you can substitute 1 cup of cooked brown rice for the uncooked cauliflower rice.

stuffed peppers

SERVES 4 / COOK TIME: 8 TO 10 HOURS ON LOW

GLUTEN-FREE

This is another traditional recipe that you might not associate with the slow cooker, but it works very well. Stuffed peppers are so easy to make and extremely versatile when it comes to ingredients. Use the protein of your choice—ground chicken, turkey, beef, or pork. For the grains, use brown rice or even quinoa. If your diet allows, you might add some cheese on top of each pepper for the last few minutes of cook time as a nice finishing touch. You'll know the peppers are done when they're soft to the touch—so soft, you can cut them with a fork.

Cooking spray

1 pound ground pork

1 cup cooked quinoa or brown rice

3 tablespoons grated Parmesan cheese

1 (15-ounce) can crushed tomatoes

3 garlic cloves, minced

2 tablespoons dried oregano

1 tablespoon dried basil

½ teaspoon salt

¼ teaspoon freshly ground black pepper

6 red or green bell peppers

....

PER SERVING Calories: 347; Total Fat: 7g; Saturated Fat: 3g; Protein: 43g; Carbohydrates: 31g; Cholesterol: 95mg; Sodium: 679mg; Fiber: 8g; Sugar: 11g

1. Coat the inside of the slow cooker with cooking spray.

2. In a large bowl, mix the ground meat, quinoa, Parmesan cheese, tomatoes, garlic, oregano, basil, salt, and pepper.

3. Slice the top off each bell pepper and scoop out the seeds. Spoon the meat filling into each bell pepper cavity.

4. Stand the bell peppers in the slow cooker.

5. Cover and cook on low for 8 to 10 hours.

Tip: As an optional step, top the cooked bell peppers with ½ cup shredded mozzarella cheese. Re-cover and cook for an additional 10 to 15 minutes, or until the cheese has melted.

beef with broccoli

SERVES 4 / COOK TIME: 8 TO 10 HOURS ON LOW

GLUTEN-FREE • PALEO • DAIRY-FREE

I love it when a healthy homemade recipe turns out better than takeout—though honestly, it's hardly surprising. Most beef and broccoli recipes use brown sugar or another sweetener. Why is this necessary? I almost added honey, but I tasted the sauce and realized it just didn't need it. I used an arrowroot powder slurry to thicken up the sauce once it was done cooking. This step is optional, but I recommend it.

2 pounds chuck steak, cut into thin strips

1 small onion, diced

1 cup low-sodium beef broth

½ cup low-sodium soy sauce, tamari, or coconut aminos

1 tablespoon toasted sesame oil

3 garlic cloves, minced

¼ teaspoon ground ginger

4 cups fresh or frozen small broccoli florets

FOR THE SLURRY (OPTIONAL)

2 tablespoons arrowroot powder

¼ cup cold water

PER SERVING Calories: 386; Total Fat: 16g; Saturated Fat: 4g; Protein: 50g; Carbohydrates: 11g; Cholesterol: 130mg; Sodium: 1,976mg; Fiber: 3g; Sugar: 5g

1. Combine the beef and onion in the slow cooker.

2. In a medium bowl, whisk together the broth, soy sauce, sesame oil, garlic, and ginger.

3. Pour the sauce into the slow cooker and stir to coat the beef well.

4. Cover and cook on low for 8 to 10 hours.

5. During the last 30 minutes of cook time, stir in the broccoli. Re-cover and finish cooking.

6. If desired, whisk together the arrowroot powder and water. Pour the slurry into the slow cooker and stir gently. Re-cover and cook for an additional 10 to 15 minutes, or until the sauce is thickened.

Tip: You can serve this dish any number of ways: over brown rice, cauliflower rice, or even mashed cauliflower or potatoes.

carne asada

SERVES 4 / COOK TIME: FOR 8 TO 10 HOURS ON LOW

GLUTEN-FREE • DAIRY-FREE

A healthy, homemade sauce cooks with flank steak, producing tender, falling-apart carne asada. If you cook the meat alone, this recipe is especially versatile: use it in tacos, burritos, enchiladas, and salads, or even to stuff sweet potatoes. But by adding corn and black beans, the recipe is transformed into a one-pot meal. You'll know the meat is done when it shreds easily with two forks.

FOR THE MEAT

1 onion, sliced

1 red or green bell pepper,
    seeded and sliced

1 (15-ounce) can corn, drained

1 cup cooked black beans,
    rinsed and drained

2 pounds flank or skirt steak

Chopped fresh cilantro, for garnish

FOR THE SAUCE

¼ cup freshly squeezed lime juice

¼ cup freshly squeezed orange juice

3 tablespoons extra-virgin olive oil

4 garlic cloves, minced

1 teaspoon ground cumin

½ teaspoon chili powder

½ teaspoon dried oregano

½ teaspoon salt

¼ teaspoon freshly ground
    black pepper

1. Combine the onion, bell pepper, corn, and black beans in the slow cooker.

2. Place the steak on top.

3. In a small bowl, whisk together all the sauce ingredients. Pour the sauce into the slow cooker, making sure all the ingredients are covered.

4. Cover and cook on low for 8 to 10 hours.

5. Garnish with fresh cilantro before serving.

Tip: I recommend using dried black beans; just be sure to soak them overnight first.

PER SERVING Calories: 573; Total Fat: 30g; Saturated Fat: 10g; Protein: 52g; Carbohydrates: 23g; Cholesterol: 150mg; Sodium: 538mg; Fiber: 4g; Sugar: 8g

beef and spinach meat loaf with fingerling potatoes

SERVES 4 / COOK TIME: 8 TO 10 HOURS ON LOW

GLUTEN-FREE • DAIRY-FREE

Meat loaf in the slow cooker? Of course. And the opportunities for variation abound: While I call for beef, you can use your preferred ground meat or combo of meats. If you can't have nuts, feel free to swap out the almond flour for bread crumbs. (If the diced tomatoes make your loaf a bit too wet, just add a little more flour or bread crumbs until it evens out.) I added chopped spinach, but you can get creative and add kale, bell pepper, or mushrooms. And of course, you can use whatever ketchup you like with this dish or even omit it altogether.

FOR THE MEAT LOAF

1 pound ground beef

1 large egg, lightly beaten

1 small onion, diced

2 garlic cloves, minced

½ cup chopped spinach

1 cup diced tomatoes

¼ cup almond flour

2 tablespoons Italian Seasoning (page 100)

1 teaspoon salt

½ teaspoon freshly ground black pepper

1 pound fingerling potatoes

FOR THE KETCHUP

1 (8-ounce) can tomato sauce

½ teaspoon distilled white vinegar

1 teaspoon Italian Seasoning (page 100)

1. In a large bowl, combine the ground beef, egg, onion, garlic, spinach, tomatoes, almond flour, Italian seasoning, salt, and pepper. Mix well and shape the meat mixture into a loaf.

2. Place the loaf in the slow cooker.

3. Add the potatoes around the loaf.

4. Cover and cook on low for 8 to 10 hours.

5. During the last 10 minutes of cook time, whisk together the ketchup ingredients and spread it on top of the meat loaf.

6. Re-cover and finish cooking.

....

PER SERVING Calories: 292; Total Fat: 15g; Saturated Fat: 5g; Protein: 22g; Carbohydrates: 18g; Cholesterol: 97mg; Sodium: 675mg; Fiber: 3g; Sugar: 4g

Tip: Can you double the recipe? Yes, but not if you're including the potatoes—there simply won't be room in the slow cooker.

beef and sweet potato casserole with bell peppers

SERVES 6 / COOK TIME: 8 TO 10 HOURS ON LOW

GLUTEN-FREE • PALEO • DAIRY-FREE

This casserole is my go-to when I need something filling but healthy. For its hearty meat and potatoes base, I use beef and sweet potatoes, with a creamy sauce that's nondairy and gluten-free. The dish is also loaded with onions, peppers, and carrots, and you can certainly add other vegetables to your liking.

1¾ pounds beef stew meat

2 pounds sweet potatoes, peeled and cut into 1-inch-thick pieces

1 (15-ounce) can full-fat coconut milk or coconut cream

1 onion, sliced

1 red or green bell pepper, seeded and sliced

2 carrots, peeled and chopped

4 garlic cloves, minced

2 teaspoons dried rosemary

1 teaspoon paprika

1 teaspoon salt

½ teaspoon freshly ground black pepper

1. Combine all the ingredients in the slow cooker and mix well.

2. Cover and cook on low for 8 to 10 hours, or until the potatoes are tender.

Tip: Even though this recipe uses coconut milk or coconut cream, you'll find this dish won't have a strong coconut flavor. It's really just used as a thickening agent.

PER SERVING Calories: 598; Total Fat: 27g; Saturated Fat: 19g; Protein: 34g; Carbohydrates: 49g; Cholesterol: 88mg; Sodium: 518mg; Fiber: 10g; Sugar: 6g

italian beef roast with artichokes and tomatoes

SERVES 6 / COOK TIME: 8 TO 10 HOURS ON LOW

GLUTEN-FREE • PALEO • DAIRY-FREE

Like chilies, roasts were made for slow cookers. They're as foolproof as it gets in slow cooking. For this reason, there are hundreds of roast recipes out there. This one, however, is more than just another beef roast—it's an entire Italian meal, complete with vegetables and starch. As for the veggies, load it up with your favorites. Tomatoes, garlic, onion, bell pepper, artichokes, and olives sounded nice to me, so I've included them here, but mushrooms, eggplant, and even asparagus would make appealing additions, too.

1 pound sweet potatoes, peeled and diced

1 red or green bell pepper, seeded and sliced

1 onion, sliced

1 (3-pound) beef roast

1 (2-ounce) can sliced black olives, drained

1 (6-ounce) jar marinated artichoke hearts, with their juice

1 (15-ounce) can diced tomatoes, with their juice

3 garlic cloves, minced

1 teaspoon salt

½ teaspoon freshly ground black pepper

½ teaspoon paprika

½ teaspoon dried basil

½ teaspoon dried oregano

½ teaspoon dried parsley

¼ teaspoon red pepper flakes

1. Combine the sweet potatoes, bell pepper, and onion in the slow cooker.

2. Place the beef roast on top of the vegetables.

3. Add the remaining ingredients on top of the roast.

4. Cover and cook on low for 8 to 10 hours.

PER SERVING Calories: 431; Total Fat: 12g; Saturated Fat: 3g; Protein: 47g; Carbohydrates: 30g; Cholesterol: 130mg; Sodium: 597mg; Fiber: 6g; Sugar: 4g

Tip: To switch things up, substitute ground beef for the roast. However, I suggest you do so only if you have time to brown the ground beef on the stove top and drain the grease first.

corned beef and cabbage

SERVES 4 / COOK TIME: 8 TO 10 HOURS ON HIGH

GLUTEN-FREE • DAIRY-FREE

Known as the traditional Irish dish for St. Patrick's Day, corned beef and cabbage is a recipe I think should be cooked year-round. Corned beef is a tough cut of meat, so it's perfectly suited to the slow cooker, but it needs to cook a bit longer—and at a higher temperature—than other cuts. So yes, you read that correctly, this cooks for 8 to 10 hours on high, not on low. The meat will become so tender it should slice very easily when you take it out.

1 pound red potatoes, cut in half

1 pound carrots, peeled and chopped

1 onion, chopped

1 (2-pound) corned beef brisket

1 cinnamon stick, broken into
    several pieces

1 teaspoon mustard seeds

1 teaspoon black peppercorns

8 whole cloves

8 whole allspice berries

12 whole juniper berries

1 bay leaf, crumbled

1 teaspoon ground ginger

4 cups water *or* 2 cups water
    plus 2 cups low-sodium broth

1 head green cabbage,
    cored and chopped

1. Put the potatoes, carrots, and onion in the slow cooker.

2. Place the corned beef brisket on top.

3. Scatter the spices on top of the meat.

4. Pour the water over everything.

5. Cover and cook on high for 8 to 10 hours.

6. In the remaining 1 hour of cook time, add the cabbage, re-cover, and finish cooking.

7. Transfer the corned beef brisket to a serving platter. Slice thinly across the grain and serve with the vegetables.

Tip: Some recipes place the meat on the bottom of the slow cooker, but I prefer my potatoes and veggies on the bottom and the meat on top. At the end of the day, it really doesn't matter.

PER SERVING Calories: 580; Total Fat: 28g; Saturated Fat: 12g; Protein: 37g; Carbohydrates: 45g; Cholesterol: 142mg; Sodium: 2,132mg; Fiber: 11g; Sugar: 15g

dairy-free beef stroganoff

SERVES 4 / COOK TIME: 6 TO 8 HOURS ON LOW

GLUTEN-FREE • DAIRY-FREE

I know when most people think of beef stroganoff, they don't necessarily think slow cooker or healthy. This recipe is both—without compromising the traditional flavor—and it's dairy-free to boot.

2 pounds sirloin steak tips, trimmed to 0% fat, cut into short, thin strips

1 onion, chopped

2 garlic cloves, minced

8 ounces mushrooms, sliced

1 cup coconut cream or full-fat coconut milk

1 cup low-sodium beef broth

2 tablespoons low-sodium soy sauce, tamari, or coconut aminos

1 teaspoon salt

½ teaspoon dried parsley

½ teaspoon onion powder

¼ teaspoon freshly ground black pepper

10 ounces egg noodles, gluten-free if desired, cooked

1. Combine the beef, onion, garlic, and mushrooms in the slow cooker.

2. In a medium bowl, whisk together the coconut cream, broth, soy sauce, and seasonings. Pour the sauce into the slow cooker and mix well.

3. Cover and cook on low 6 to 8 hours.

4. Stir in the cooked egg noodles before serving.

Tip: If you'd like to thicken up your stroganoff, whisk 2 tablespoons of arrowroot powder into ¼ cup of cold water. Pour the mixture into the slow cooker before adding the noodles, stir, and heat for 15 minutes, or until thickened to your liking.

PER SERVING Calories: 597; Total Fat: 18g; Saturated Fat: 7g; Protein: 58g; Carbohydrates: 30g; Cholesterol: 100mg; Sodium: 1,011mg; Fiber: 5g; Sugar: 7g

lamb shepherd's pie

SERVES 4 / COOK TIME: 8 TO 10 HOURS ON LOW

GLUTEN-FREE • PALEO

There are so many different versions of "traditional" shepherd's pie. To me, this is one of those recipes you should tweak to your liking. Don't have thyme? Use rosemary instead. Don't like peas? Substitute diced zucchini. If you like, you can even swap out the mashed cauliflower for mashed sweet potatoes, or create a mixture of the two.

FOR THE PIE

1 pound ground or chopped lamb

1 onion, diced

2 garlic cloves, minced

½ cup peas or 2 zucchini, diced

½ cup chopped carrots

⅓ cup low-sodium beef broth

2 tablespoons tomato paste

2 tablespoons almond flour (optional)

1½ teaspoons salt

1 teaspoon dried thyme

½ teaspoon freshly ground
   black pepper

FOR THE MASHED CAULIFLOWER

1 pound cauliflower florets, steamed

1 teaspoon ghee

2 to 3 tablespoons unsweetened
   almond milk (or more)

½ teaspoon salt

¼ teaspoon freshly ground
   black pepper

Brown: In a large skillet, brown the ground lamb over medium heat. Drain off the grease.

1. Combine all the pie ingredients, including the browned lamb, in the slow cooker and mix well.

2. Cover and cook on low for 8 to 10 hours.

3. During the last 30 minutes of cook time, combine the cauliflower, ghee, almond milk, salt, and pepper in a food processor and pulse until smooth, adding more almond milk if necessary.

4. Spread the mashed cauliflower on top of the pie filling, re-cover, and finish cooking.

Tip: This recipe contains no cheese, and it's not cooked in the oven, so don't be surprised that the mashed topping doesn't crisp up.

PER SERVING Calories: 378; Total Fat: 25g; Saturated Fat: 11g; Protein: 24g; Carbohydrates: 17g; Cholesterol: 88mg; Sodium: 1,311mg; Fiber: 6g; Sugar: 7g

lamb and apricot tagine with chickpeas

SERVES 6 / COOK TIME: 8 TO 10 HOURS ON LOW

GLUTEN-FREE • DAIRY-FREE

A tagine is a North African stew of highly spiced meat and vegetables—it's named for the ceramic pot in which it's traditionally cooked. This slow cooker tagine is one of the most flavorful recipes in this cookbook. This dish is high in protein, while the apricots add a nice fruity touch. Of course, the rest of the ingredients are natural, as well.

3 pounds bone-in lamb shanks

1 (15-ounce) can chickpeas, rinsed and drained

1 (15-ounce) can diced tomatoes, with their juice

2½ cups low-sodium chicken broth

1 large onion, diced

4 garlic cloves, minced

¾ cup halved dried apricots

1 teaspoon ground ginger

1 teaspoon ground cumin

1 teaspoon ground turmeric

1 teaspoon paprika

1 teaspoon red pepper flakes

½ teaspoon ground cinnamon

½ teaspoon ground coriander

½ teaspoon ground nutmeg

½ teaspoon ground cloves

½ teaspoon salt

½ teaspoon freshly ground black pepper

Fresh herb of your choice, for garnish

1. Combine all the ingredients in the slow cooker and mix well.

2. Cover and cook on low for 8 to 10 hours.

3. Garnish with a fresh herb of your choice before serving.

....

PER SERVING Calories: 536; Total Fat: 21g; Saturated Fat: 9g; Protein: 37g; Carbohydrates: 41g; Cholesterol: 106mg; Sodium: 614mg; Fiber: 5g; Sugar: 19g

Tip: A tagine is traditionally served over couscous but also works well over rice.

Lemon Cake *page 156*

sweets

. . . .

poached pears

SERVES 4 / COOK TIME: 3 TO 5 HOURS ON LOW

GLUTEN-FREE • VEGETARIAN • PALEO • DAIRY-FREE

I put this fruity treat in my slow cooker as soon as my dinner guests arrive. That way it's warmed up just in time to serve for dessert. I think my guests appreciate that this is not just flavorful but healthy—when combined, ginger and cinnamon provide antibacterial elements that protect the body from ailments and improve your general well-being. The only prep involved is mixing up the sauce. It's not stirred over heat, so the honey may clump up in the apple juice as you whisk. Just keep whisking until the honey is completely dissolved.

4 pears, peeled, cored, and halved

½ cup apple juice

¼ cup honey or maple syrup

½ teaspoon vanilla extract

½ teaspoon grated lemon zest

2 teaspoons ground cinnamon

½ teaspoon ground ginger

. . . .

PER SERVING Calories: 205; Total Fat: 0g; Saturated Fat: 0g; Protein: 1g; Carbohydrates: 54g; Cholesterol: 0g; Sodium: 5mg; Fiber: 7g; Sugar: 41g

1. Place the pear halves in the slow cooker, cut-side up.

2. In a small bowl, whisk together the apple juice, honey, vanilla, lemon zest, cinnamon, and ginger. Pour the sauce on top of the pears.

3. Cover and cook on low for 3 to 5 hours.

Tip: The number of pears you can make will depend on the size of your slow cooker.

paleo mixed fruit compote

SERVES 6 / COOK TIME: 5 TO 7 HOURS ON LOW

GLUTEN-FREE • VEGETARIAN • PALEO • DAIRY-FREE

I try to eat berries as often as possible: These nutrition powerhouses are good sources of fiber, excellent for the digestive system, and full of antioxidants that fight stress and illness. Using four varieties in this compote provides the perfect way to increase your berry intake! Serve hot or cold, spooned over ice cream or even brownies—or for breakfast as a topping for French toast or pancakes. I usually eat it by itself or add a few tablespoons to my morning smoothie. To experiment with other flavors, you can try a different combination of fruit, as long as the amounts stay the same.

8 ounces blueberries, chopped

8 ounces strawberries, chopped

8 ounces raspberries, chopped

8 ounces blackberries, chopped

½ cup honey or maple syrup

1 tablespoon freshly squeezed
   lemon juice

2 teaspoons chia seeds

½ teaspoon ground cinnamon

....

PER SERVING Calories: 164; Total Fat: 1g;
Saturated Fat: 0g; Protein: 2g;
Carbohydrates: 40g; Cholesterol: 0mg;
Sodium: 8mg; Fiber: 7g; Sugar: 32g

1. Combine all the ingredients in the slow cooker and mix well.

2. Cover and cook on low 5 to 7 hours.

Tip: Keep in mind that the compote will thicken naturally as it sets overnight, but you can omit the chia seeds if you don't want a thick compote. Store in the refrigerator for up to 2 weeks.

5-ingredient blueberry applesauce

SERVES 6 / COOK TIME: 4 TO 6 HOURS ON LOW

GLUTEN-FREE • VEGETARIAN • PALEO • DAIRY-FREE

I love pairing two different fruits when making applesauce. There are tons of potential variations like apple-pear and apple-cranberry, but this one is my favorite. If your blueberries aren't particularly sweet, your batch may be a sweet and tangy mix. If so, don't assume you must add more honey! This tang can be delicious as is. More important, don't peel the apples! That's where all the nutrients are. The skins will cook down so soft you'll never know they were even there.

1½ pounds apples, cored and diced

4 ounces blueberries

2 tablespoons water

1 tablespoon honey or maple syrup

1 teaspoon ground cinnamon

....

PER SERVING Calories: 103; Total Fat: 0g; Saturated Fat: 0g; Protein: 1g; Carbohydrates: 27g; Cholesterol: 0mg; Sodium: 2mg; Fiber: 4g; Sugar: 21g

1. Combine all the ingredients in the slow cooker and mix well.

2. Cover and cook on low 4 to 6 hours.

3. Use an immersion blender or food processor to blend until you achieve the desired consistency.

Tip: An alternative to honey or maple syrup is pitted dates. Dates are a great natural sweetener. Like the apple skins, they will cook down so soft you won't notice their skins.

cinnamon apples

SERVES 6 / COOK TIME: 4 TO 6 HOURS ON LOW

GLUTEN-FREE • VEGETARIAN • PALEO • DAIRY-FREE

Sometimes I like to whip up a batch of these apples just so my kitchen will be filled with the tantalizing aroma of apples cooking down low and slow, mixed with cinnamon and honey. It's one of the simplest recipes in this cookbook, but that doesn't mean it won't taste just as good as the others. Depending on your dietary needs, you can choose between chia seeds and arrowroot powder.

6 apples, peeled, cored and
  thinly sliced

1 cup honey or maple syrup

1 tablespoon ground cinnamon

3 tablespoons arrowroot starch
  or 1 tablespoon chia seeds

⅛ teaspoon salt

. . . .

PER SERVING Calories: 306; Total Fat: 0g;
Saturated Fat: 0g; Protein: 1g;
Carbohydrates: 82g; Cholesterol: 0mg;
Sodium: 392mg; Fiber: 6g; Sugar: 70g

1. Combine all the ingredients in the slow cooker and mix well.

2. Cover and cook on low for 4 to 6 hours.

3. Stir and serve warm.

Tip: I like to use sweet apples like Gala or Red Delicious. This is equally delicious served alone or as a topping on ice cream, pie, cobbler, or pancakes.

cranberry-walnut stuffed apples

SERVES 6 / COOK TIME: 4 TO 6 HOURS ON LOW

GLUTEN-FREE • VEGETARIAN • PALEO • DAIRY-FREE

This dessert not only tastes great, but it's fun to put together. You can even involve the kids for a family-friendly activity. It's good for you, too—stuffed with healthy nuts, which are packed with protein, fiber, vitamin E, omega-3 fatty acids, and unsaturated fats. Of course, you can replace the walnuts with pecans or almond, if you prefer. Not a fan of cranberries? Use raisins or another dried fruit. Vegan? Use maple syrup instead of honey. Have the kids load these up and pop them in the slow cooker.

¼ cup water

6 apples

10 ounces walnuts, chopped

4 ounces dried cranberries

2 teaspoons honey or maple syrup

¼ teaspoon ground cinnamon

....

PER SERVING Calories: 466; Total Fat: 31g; Saturated Fat: 3g; Protein: 8g; Carbohydrates: 39g; Cholesterol: 0mg; Sodium: 3mg; Fiber: 9g; Sugar: 27g

1. Pour the water into the slow cooker.

2. Use an apple corer to remove the core almost all the way to the bottom of each apple. (If you don't have an apple corer, first cut out a circle around the top of each apple with a knife. Then use a melon baller or small spoon to scoop out the core almost down to the bottom.)

3. In a small bowl, combine the walnuts, cranberries, honey, and cinnamon, and mix well.

4. Stuff the apples equally with the mixture.

5. Place the apples in the slow cooker.

6. Cover and cook on low for 4 to 6 hours, or until the apples become soft.

Tip: These stuffed apples are delicious served with whipped topping.

ginger-vanilla pears

SERVES 4 / COOK TIME: 3 TO 5 HOURS ON LOW

GLUTEN-FREE • VEGETARIAN • PALEO • DAIRY-FREE

This is a recipe I pull out when I want to impress dinner guests but don't have a lot of time. Thanks to this dessert, your entire house will also smell fantastic. And it will look like you put a great deal of effort into its preparation. As a bonus, pears are one of the lower-calorie fruits and a great source of dietary fiber, so this can double as a good weight-loss snack.

2 pears, halved and cored

¼ cup honey or maple syrup

½ teaspoon vanilla extract

½ teaspoon ground ginger

⅛ teaspoon ground cinnamon

1 teaspoon ghee or vegetable oil

PER SERVING Calories: 137; Total Fat: 1g; Saturated Fat: 1g; Protein: 1g; Carbohydrates: 34g; Cholesterol: 2mg; Sodium: 3mg; Fiber: 3g; Sugar: 28g

1. Place the pear halves in the bottom of the slow cooker, cut-side up.

2. In a small bowl, whisk together the honey, vanilla, ginger, and cinnamon. Pour the sauce on top of the pears.

3. Add ¼ teaspoon of the ghee to each pear half.

4. Cover and cook on low for 3 to 5 hours.

Tip: Chopped pecans or walnuts or almond slivers are great toppings for this dessert. Adding a bit of grated cheese can provide another tasty spin.

campfire banana boats

SERVES 4 / COOK TIME: 3 TO 5 HOURS ON LOW

GLUTEN-FREE • VEGETARIAN • DAIRY-FREE

I think it's safe to say that anyone who has ever gone camping has tasted a banana boat. It's a campfire classic—and rightfully so. However, there's no reason you have to wait to go camping for this kid-friendly dessert. Just throw it in the slow cooker!

4 bananas, unpeeled

½ cup vegan chocolate chips

½ cup rolled oats

1 teaspoon honey or maple syrup

½ cup miniature marshmallows (optional)

....

PER SERVING Calories: 155; Total Fat: 3g; Saturated Fat: 1g; Protein: 2g; Carbohydrates: 34g; Cholesterol: 0mg; Sodium: 6mg; Fiber: 4g; Sugar: 20g

1. Cut 4 (12-inch) sheets of aluminum foil.

2. Make a deep lengthwise cut along the inside curve of each banana, but don't cut all the way through.

3. Open the slit to form a pocket, and fill each banana with 2 tablespoons chocolate chips, 2 tablespoons oats, and ¼ teaspoon honey.

4. Wrap each banana in foil and seal at the top.

5. Place the bananas in the slow cooker.

6. Cover and cook on low for 3 to 5 hours. Note: The foil will become extremely hot, so use oven mitts when removing the boats from the slow cooker.

7. Top with marshmallows, if using.

Tip: For a healthy marshmallow, I recommend natural vegan Dandies brand. They contain no high-fructose corn syrup and are Non-GMO Project Verified.

paleo apple pie filling

SERVES 4 / COOK TIME: 3 TO 5 HOURS ON LOW

GLUTEN-FREE • VEGETARIAN • PALEO • DAIRY-FREE

Not quite an apple pie but halfway there, this Paleo apple pie filling has no added sugar! This filling is so versatile, you don't even have to use it for a pie at all. It makes a great dessert, or you can even eat it for breakfast. Honey (or maple syrup) is used to sweeten the filling; without it, it will be very tart.

8 cups died apples

1 tablespoon freshly squeezed lemon juice

1¼ cups water

3 tablespoons honey or maple syrup

3 tablespoons chia seeds

1½ teaspoons ground cinnamon

¼ teaspoon ground nutmeg

. . . .

PER SERVING Calories: 320; Total Fat: 5g; Saturated Fat: 1g; Protein: 4g; Carbohydrates: 73g; Cholesterol: 0mg; Sodium: 118mg; Fiber: 15g; Sugar: 58g

1. Combine the apples and lemon juice in the slow cooker.

2. In a medium bowl, whisk together the water, honey, chia seeds, cinnamon, and nutmeg. Pour the mixture over the apples and mix well.

3. Cover and cook on low for 3 to 5 hours, or until the apples are tender.

Tip: I like to use sweeter apples for this recipe, so I usually go with Gala or Red Delicious.

rice pudding

SERVES 4 / COOK TIME: 4 TO 5 HOURS ON LOW

GLUTEN-FREE • VEGETARIAN

Rice pudding in the slow cooker is a real treat. But this can be a finicky recipe at first, until you get the hang of it. Depending on how your slow cooker heats, rice pudding can quickly overcook, producing a dry, inedible result. Once you've gotten it down, though, this pudding is sure to become a favorite—and provides a great choice for a gluten-free dessert, too.

Cooking spray

¾ cup long-grain rice

3 cups unsweetened almond milk

¾ cup honey or maple syrup

1 tablespoon ghee

1 teaspoon vanilla extract

½ teaspoon ground cinnamon

¼ teaspoon salt

....

PER SERVING Calories: 416; Total Fat: 8g; Saturated Fat: 2g; Protein: 5g; Carbohydrates: 82g; Cholesterol: 8mg; Sodium: 422mg; Fiber: 3g; Sugar: 52g

1. Coat the slow cooker generously with cooking spray.

2. Combine all the ingredients in the slow cooker and mix well.

3. Cover and cook on low for 4 to 5 hours.

> **Tip:** Keep extra almond milk on hand, as you might need it to thin out the rice pudding if it's too thick for your taste.

peach cobbler

SERVES 4 / COOK TIME: 4 TO 5 HOURS ON LOW

GLUTEN-FREE • VEGETARIAN

Oats are one of the healthiest grains on earth. In addition to being naturally gluten-free, they are a good source of fiber and antioxidants. Grinding your own oat flour is an easy way to make your own healthy flour. All you do is put the rolled oats in a food processor and grind until they reach your desired consistency. I keep a bin of oat flour in my pantry for recipes like this.

FOR THE COBBLER

Cooking spray

1½ cups oat flour (rolled oats ground to flour consistency)

2 to 3 tablespoons unsweetened almond milk

2 tablespoons honey or maple syrup

1 teaspoon vanilla extract

1 teaspoon ground cinnamon

1 teaspoon baking powder

¼ teaspoon salt

FOR THE PEACHES

6 cups sliced peaches

⅓ cup honey or maple syrup

1 teaspoon vanilla extract

1 tablespoon ghee

1. Coat the slow cooker lightly with cooking spray.

2. In a medium bowl, whisk together all the cobbler ingredients.

3. Crumble the cobbler mixture evenly over the bottom of the slow cooker.

4. In another medium bowl, toss the peaches with the honey and vanilla. Pour the fruit on top of the cobbler dough.

5. Dot the ghee evenly over the top.

6. Cover and cook on low for 4 to 5 hours, or until the juices are bubbling.

Tip: If you like, you can swap out the peaches for another fruit or berry. Strawberries and blueberries work especially well.

PER SERVING Calories: 206; Total Fat: 5g; Saturated Fat: 2g; Protein: 4g; Carbohydrates: 39g; Cholesterol: 8mg; Sodium: 174mg; Fiber: 5g; Sugar: 30g

berry crisp

SERVES 4 / COOK TIME: 2 TO 3 HOURS ON LOW

GLUTEN-FREE • VEGAN • DAIRY-FREE

There are only two ingredients in this recipe—or three if you want to add a natural sweetener like honey or maple syrup. Depending on what type of granola you use and how sweet your berries are, you may not need a sweetener at all. If you're using store-bought granola, be sure to check the ingredients label for sugar or other sweeteners.

Cooking spray

6 cups of your favorite berries

2 cups Dried Fruit and Nut Granola (page 18) or other favorite granola

....

PER SERVING Calories: 211; Total Fat: 2g; Saturated Fat: 0g; Protein: 5g; Carbohydrates: 44g; Cholesterol: 0mg; Sodium: 3mg; Fiber: 10g; Sugar: 18g

1. Coat the slow cooker generously with cooking spray.

2. Spread the berries in the bottom of the slow cooker.

3. Scatter the granola over the top.

4. Lay a dish towel or one to two paper towels between the slow cooker and the lid. This will absorb all the condensation so it won't drip back onto the granola while it cooks.

5. Cover and cook on low for 2 to 3 hours, or until the juices are bubbling.

Tip: The variations are endless—you can honestly use any combo of berries you please, but I recommend choosing berries that are naturally sweet.

peach crisp

SERVES 4 / COOK TIME: 2 TO 3 HOURS ON LOW

GLUTEN-FREE • VEGAN • DAIRY-FREE

If this recipe looks familiar, that's because it's the same as my Berry Crisp recipe (page 152). All I did was replace the berries with fresh peaches. The same recommendations apply—depending on which granola you choose and how sweet your peaches are, you may or may not need to add a touch of honey or maple syrup.

Cooking spray

6 cups sliced peaches

2 cups Dried Fruit and Nut Granola
(page 18) or other favorite granola

....

PER SERVING Calories: 180; Total Fat: 2g;
Saturated Fat: 0g; Protein: 5g;
Carbohydrates: 39g; Cholesterol: 0mg;
Sodium: 3mg; Fiber: 5g; Sugar: 24g

1. Coat your slow cooker generously with cooking spray.

2. Spread the peaches in the bottom of the slow cooker.

3. Scatter the granola over the top.

4. Lay a dish towel or one to two paper towels between the slow cooker and the lid. This will absorb all the condensation so it won't drip back onto the granola while it cooks.

5. Cover and cook on low for 2 to 3 hours, or until the juices are bubbling.

Tip: Try to find very ripe peaches to use in this recipe. To hasten ripening, place the peaches in a brown paper bag on the counter for 24 to 48 hours.

apple-oatmeal crisp

SERVES 4 / COOK TIME: 2 TO 3 HOURS ON LOW

GLUTEN-FREE • VEGETARIAN • DAIRY-FREE

This recipe is part cobbler, part crisp—the best of both worlds. It's 100 percent certain your kitchen will smell out-of-this-world good. Depending on how your slow cooker heats up, you may need to adjust the cooking time. You'll know it's done when you see the juices bubbling through the oatmeal topping.

Cooking spray

6 cups diced apples

¼ cup apple juice

2 cups rolled oats

2 tablespoons honey or maple syrup

1 teaspoon vanilla extract

1 teaspoon ground cinnamon

¼ teaspoon salt

. . . .

PER SERVING Calories: 253; Total Fat: 1g; Saturated Fat: 0g; Protein: 2g; Carbohydrates: 65g; Cholesterol: 0g; Sodium: 152mg; Fiber: 10g; Sugar: 49g

1. Coat the slow cooker generously with cooking spray.

2. Combine the apples and juice in the slow cooker.

3. Scatter the rolled oats evenly over the top.

4. Drizzle the honey, vanilla, cinnamon, and salt on top of the oats.

5. Lay a dish towel or one to two paper towels between the slow cooker and the lid. This will absorb all the condensation so it won't drip back onto the oats while it cooks.

6. Cover and cook on low for 2 to 3 hours, or until the juices are bubbling and tender.

Tip: While you can use any type of apple for this dessert, I would suggest a sweet apple like Red Delicious, Fuji, Gala, or Golden Delicious.

banana bread

SERVES 6 / COOK TIME: 2 TO 4 HOURS ON LOW

GLUTEN-FREE • VEGETARIAN

Bread? Of course bread can be cooked in the slow cooker. I'm not much of a plain bread person—in general, when the basket is going around, I pass. Banana bread, on the other hand, I can never resist. I can eat an entire pan if it's placed in front of me. And when prepared in the slow cooker, banana bread is extra moist.

Cooking spray

¼ cup ghee, melted

2 large eggs

½ cup honey

1 teaspoon baking powder

½ teaspoon baking soda

½ teaspoon salt

2½ cups almond flour

4 very ripe bananas, mashed

....

PER SERVING Calories: 327; Total Fat: 17g; Saturated Fat: 6g; Protein: 6g; Carbohydrates: 44g; Cholesterol: 84mg; Sodium: 326mg; Fiber: 3g; Sugar: 33g

1. Coat the slow cooker generously with cooking spray.

2. In a large bowl, whisk together the ghee, eggs, honey, baking powder, baking soda, and salt until well combined

3. Stir in the almond flour and mashed bananas.

4. Pour the batter into the slow cooker.

5. Lay a dish towel or one to two paper towels between the slow cooker and the lid. This will absorb all the condensation so it won't drip back onto the batter while it cooks.

6. Cover and cook on low for 2 to 4 hours.

Tip: Since this banana bread can overcook quickly, I suggest you watch as it cooks the first time you prepare it, to ensure it doesn't dry out or burn. You'll know it's done when a toothpick inserted in the center comes out clean.

lemon cake

SERVES 6 / COOK TIME: 2 TO 4 HOURS ON LOW

GLUTEN-FREE • VEGETARIAN

I really tried to make this cake as healthy as possible, but at the end of the day, it's a cake. If you look at the ingredients, you'll notice they lean toward Paleo, but this is not a full Paleo cake, as it includes baking powder. Making this 100 percent Paleo, however, is simple: Just whisk together 2 teaspoons cream of tartar and 1 teaspoon baking soda in a small bowl, and substitute this "Paleo baking powder" for the store-bought kind.

Cooking spray

1½ cups almond flour

½ cup coconut flour

2 teaspoons baking powder

½ cup coconut cream

⅓ cup ghee, melted

Juice and grated zest of 1 lemon

2 small eggs

3 tablespoons honey

....

PER SERVING Calories: 251; Total Fat: 14g; Saturated Fat: 9g; Protein: 9g; Carbohydrates: 26g; Cholesterol: 46mg; Sodium: 45mg; Fiber: 10g; Sugar: 12g

1. Coat the slow cooker generously with cooking spray.

2. In a medium bowl, whisk together all the ingredients until smooth.

3. Pour the batter into the slow cooker.

4. Lay a dish towel or one to two paper towels between the slow cooker and the lid. This will absorb all the condensation so it won't drip back onto the batter while it cooks.

5. Cover and cook on low for 2 to 4 hours.

Tip: The cook time is just a guide; the cake is done when a toothpick inserted in the center comes out clean.

bread pudding

SERVES 6 / COOK TIME: 3 TO 5 HOURS ON LOW

VEGETARIAN

This slow cooker adaptation of classic bread pudding is sweet with just the right amount of savory, and healthy without compromising flavor. There is room for adaptation, too. Feel free to swap the pecans for your favorite nuts and the raisins for other dried fruit. The glaze requires a little extra effort, but it finishing off this dessert wonderfully and is well worth it.

FOR THE BREAD PUDDING

Cooking spray

3 eggs

½ cup honey or pure maple syrup

2 tablespoon cinnamon

1 teaspoon nutmeg

1 cup coconut cream

1 cup almond milk

1 teaspoon vanilla

3 tablespoons ghee, melted

⅓ cup raisins

¼ cup pecans, chopped

1 loaf whole wheat bread,
   cut into 1-inch cubes

FOR THE GLAZE (OPTIONAL)

2 teaspoon coconut oil

2 teaspoon honey or
   pure maple syrup

2 teaspoon almond milk

1 teaspoon pure vanilla extract

Zest of 1 lemon or lime

1. Coat the slow cooker generously with cooking spray.

2. In a medium bowl, whisk together the eggs, honey, cinnamon, nutmeg, almond milk, coconut cream, vanilla, and ghee. Pour the mixture into the slow cooker.

3. Add the bread cubes, raisins, and pecans. Stir gently until egg mixture completely coats the bread cubes.

4. Cover and cook on low for 3 to 5 hours, until the center is firm.

5. Prepare the glaze (optional): In a small saucepan over low heat, combine all the ingredients for the glaze and cook for 2 to 4 minutes, until simmering. Remove from heat and cool.

6. Pour the glaze over the top of the bread pudding if using and serve.

Tip: The cook time for this recipe may vary depending on your slow cooker. If you find that the center is not setting, turn the slow cooker on high for 30 minutes or so.

PER SERVING Calories: 456; Total Fat: 21g; Saturated Fat: 14g; Protein: 12g; Carbohydrates: 59g; Cholesterol: 97mg; Sodium: 330mg; Fiber: 7g; Sugar: 34g

the dirty dozen
and the clean fifteen

A nonprofit environmental watchdog organization called Environmental Working Group (EWG) looks at data supplied by the U.S. Department of Agriculture (USDA) and the Food and Drug Administration (FDA) about pesticide residues. Each year it compiles a list of the best and worst pesticide loads found in commercial crops. You can use these lists to decide which fruits and vegetables to buy organic to minimize your exposure to pesticides and which produce is considered safe enough to buy conventionally. This does not mean they are pesticide-free, though, so wash these fruits and vegetables thoroughly.

Dirty Dozen

Apples	Nectarines	Spinach
Celery	Peaches	Strawberries
Cherries	Pears	Sweet Bell Peppers
Grapes	Potatoes	Tomatoes

In addition to the Dirty Dozen, the EWG added one type of produce contaminated with highly toxic organophosphate insecticides:

Hot peppers

Clean Fifteen

Asparagus	Eggplant	Onions
Avocados	Grapefruit	Papayas
Cabbage	Honeydew	Pineapples
Cantaloupes (domestic)	Kiwis	Sweet Corn
Cauliflower	Mangoes	Sweet Peas (frozen)

measurement conversions

VOLUME EQUIVALENTS (LIQUID)

US STANDARD	US STANDARD (OUNCES)	METRIC (APPROXIMATE)
2 tablespoons	1 fl. oz.	30 mL
¼ cup	2 fl. oz.	60 mL
½ cup	4 fl. oz.	120 mL
1 cup	8 fl. oz.	240 mL
1½ cups	12 fl. oz.	355 mL
2 cups or 1 pint	16 fl. oz.	475 mL
4 cups or 1 quart	32 fl. oz.	1 L
1 gallon	128 fl. oz.	4 L

OVEN TEMPERATURES

FAHRENHEIT (F)	CELSIUS (C) (APPROXIMATE)
250°F	120°C
300°F	150°C
325°F	165°C
350°F	180°C
375°F	190°C
400°F	200°C
425°F	220°C
450°F	230°C

VOLUME EQUIVALENTS (DRY)

US STANDARD	METRIC (APPROXIMATE)
⅛ teaspoon	0.5 mL
¼ teaspoon	1 mL
½ teaspoon	2 mL
¾ teaspoon	4 mL
1 teaspoon	5 mL
1 tablespoon	15 mL
¼ cup	59 mL
⅓ cup	79 mL
½ cup	118 mL
⅔ cup	156 mL
¾ cup	177 mL
1 cup	235 mL
2 cups or 1 pint	475 mL
3 cups	700 mL
4 cups or 1 quart	1 L

WEIGHT EQUIVALENTS

US STANDARD	METRIC (APPROXIMATE)
½ ounce	15 g
1 ounce	30 g
2 ounces	60 g
4 ounces	115 g
8 ounces	225 g
12 ounces	340 g
16 ounces or 1 pound	455 g

recipe index

index

· ·

acknowledgments

To my husband, Lawrence: There's no other person with whom I'd rather ride this roller coaster of life. Thank you for loving me, encouraging me, and supporting me while I follow my dreams.

To my mother: Thank you for inspiring me my entire life. I hope to one day be half the woman and cook that you are.

To my father: Thank you for always believing in me, even when I didn't believe in myself.

To Shawn and Stephan: SKS for life. Love you two.

To Dad E.: I'll forever try to impress you. Thank you for being my number one fan.

To all my family and friends who have supported me, whether by playing taste-tester or subscribing to my newsletters: I absolutely would not be here without you. Your support means everything—even when I don't say it.

To all my blog readers: I would never have believed my little old blog would blossom into a career in food writing. It wouldn't have happened without you. My sincere thanks to all of you wherever you may be.

To the team at Callisto Media: Writing this cookbook has not only been a dream come true but an incredibly rewarding experience. It's been a pleasure working with you all. A special thank-you to Elizabeth for bringing this opportunity to my plate and to Talia and Abigail for being the kindest, best editors a first-time cookbook writer could ask for.

about the author

....

Shannon Epstein is the writer behind the blog *Fit Slow Cooker Queen* (FitSlowCookerQueen.com), which specializes in healthy slow cooker recipes that use sustainable ingredients and are simple to prepare. Shannon is also known as Tweet, the writer behind Tweet.Eat.Travel. (TweetEatTravel.com), a travel review and lifestyle blog. Shannon lives in Los Angeles with her husband.